1978

University of St. Francis
GEN 821.31 S748mz
Spenser, Edmund

S0-BRF-591

3 0301 00089103 2

NELSON'S
MEDIEVAL AND RENAISSANCE
LIBRARY

General Editor
GEOFFREY SHEPHERD, M.A.
Senior Lecturer in English
University of Birmingham

Editorial Board

GEOFFREY SHEPHERD, M.A.
D. S. BREWER, M.A., PH.D.
E. G. STANLEY, M.A., PH.D.

EDMUND SPENSER

The Mutabilitie Cantos

Edited by

S. P. ZITNER, PH.D.

Professor of English
Grinnell College

LIBRARY
College of St. Francis
JOLIET, ILL.

NELSON

THOMAS NELSON AND SONS LTD

36 Park Street London W1
P.O. Box 2187 Accra
P.O. Box 336 Apapa Lagos
P.O. Box 25012 Nairobi
P.O. Box 21149 Dar es Salaam
77 Coffee Street San Fernando Trinidad

THOMAS NELSON (AUSTRALIA) LTD
597 Little Collins Street Melbourne C1

THOMAS NELSON AND SONS (SOUTH AFRICA) (PROPRIETARY) LTD
51 Commissioner Street Johannesburg

THOMAS NELSON AND SONS (CANADA) LTD
81 Curlew Drive Don Mills Ontario

THOMAS NELSON AND SONS
Copewood and Davis Streets Camden New Jersey 08103

© Thomas Nelson and Sons Ltd
and S. P. ZITNER 1968

First published 1968

17 173111 5

Printed in Great Britain by
Thomas Nelson (Printers) Ltd, London and Edinburgh

821.31
8748mg

CONTENTS

8 36 40

ACKNOWLEDGMENTS

For various kinds of advice and patience, I wish to thank the Editors of this Series, Professor Denton Fox, my colleague Professor Malcolm Nelson, and the staffs of the Newberry and Grinnell College libraries. Especially am I indebted to Dr Lawrence Towner, the Director of the Newberry, who permitted the use of materials on which this text is based and to Miss Annette Gould, who helped prepare the manuscript for the press.

ABBREVIATIONS

De Re. Nat.	Lucretius, *De Rerum Naturae* trans R. E. Latham (1951)
ELH	*English Literary History*
FQ	Spenser, *The Faerie Queene*
JAAC	*Journal of Aesthetics and Art Criticism*
JEGP	*Journal of English and Germanic Philology*
Met.	Ovid, *Metamorphoses,* trans. M. Innes (1961)
MLN	*Modern Language Notes*
MLQ	*Modern Language Quarterly*
N&Q	*Notes and Queries*
OED	*Oxford English Dictionary*
PL	Milton, *Paradise Lost*
PMLA	*Publications of the Modern Language Association of America*
RES	*Review of English Studies*
SP	*Studies in Philology*
Theog.	Hesiod, *Theogony,* trans. N. O. Brown (1953)
UTQ	*University of Toronto Quarterly*
Variorum	*The Works of Edmund Spenser: A Variorum Edition,* ed. E. Greenlaw, C. G. Osgood, F. M. Padelford R. Heffner, 10 vols. (1932–57)

INTRODUCTION

A DECADE after Spenser's death in 1599, Matthew Lownes, bookseller in St Dunstan's Churchyard, Fleet Street, brought out a folio edition of *The Faerie Queene*. It contained, in addition to six books of the epic published earlier, '*Two Cantos of Mutabilitie: Which, both for Forme and Matter, appeare to be parcell of some following Booke of the Faerie Queene, Vnder The Legend of Constancie. Neuer before imprinted.*' How and where Lownes came by the two *Cantos* and in what form, by what authority they were numbered, why a third was set off as 'unperfite', and on what basis they were associated with a Legend of Constancie—these are questions that have defied inquiry. Though the *Cantos* are obviously a fragment of *The Faerie Queene*, gathering and tying off threads of theme and feeling from the rest of the epic, they depend directly on no other passage. Far from being 'unperfite', the *Cantos* are a part more nearly complete than the whole epic. For Courthope they were 'the most sublime part' of the poem. It is as though the poet, a refugee from the rout in Ireland, and nearing death, had achieved in the *Cantos* a literary Pisgah-sight, not only in their theme, but in their resolution of the master-work he would never finish.

LIFE

This perhaps suspiciously poignant account accords with the biographical facts and with inferences we can draw from the *Cantos* themselves. Of Spenser's life we know somewhat less than has been written. We no longer believe that allowances given him at Cambridge indicate penury or illness; or that his associations there at Pembroke Hall confirm 'advanced'

Puritan or Calvinist leanings for which he was later sent to Ireland by Leicester as punishment; or that he died in London destitute and neglected. We now doubt that Spenser's phrase in a letter to his friend Gabriel Harvey ('some use of familiarity'), points to intimacy with Sir Philip Sidney, let alone membership in any hypothetical Sidney 'circle'. Increasingly, Spenser's career seems less interesting than his achievement.[1]

Edmund Spenser was born in London in 1554 or shortly before that into a modest family with Warwickshire and noble Northamptonshire connections. He was educated at the Merchant Taylors' School in London and at Pembroke Hall, Cambridge; then became secretary to his former Cambridge master, the Bishop of Rochester, and several years later entered the service of the Earl of Leicester. From perhaps 1580 to shortly before his death he was in almost continuous employment in Ireland in a variety of civil posts. These are the surface facts. Beneath them are more significant currents: the deepening of powers peculiarly suited to epic—a process from which the shorter works (the marriage odes and *Amoretti* excepted), were distractions published out of a beginner's or an exile's need; and the deepening of a conservative Anglicanism, elaborated but unaltered by experience and artistic effort. In Spenser's life as poet and thinker there is neither discovery nor conversion. The even tenor of his progress explains in part our difficulty in dating the *Cantos*.

DATE OF COMPOSITION

The *Cantos* were published in 1609, posthumously and last among Spenser's works. They confront moral abstractions in

[1] The most extensive biography is A. C. Judson, *The Life of Edmund Spenser* (1945). On the points mentioned above see D. Hamer, 'Edmund Spenser's Gown and Shilling', *RES* 23 (1947), 218–25; Virgil K. Whitaker, *The Religious Basis of Spenser's Thought*, Stanford *Studies in Language and Literature* 7 (1950); E. Rosenberg, *Leicester, Patron of Letters* (1955); J. W. Bennett, 'Did Spenser Starve', *MLN* 52 (1937), 400–1, and H. Berry and E. K. Timings, 'Spenser's Pension', *RES*, n.s. 11 (1960), 254–9, and *The Poems of Sir Philip Sidney*, ed. William A. Ringler, Jr. (1962), pp. 31–2.

a way that suggests the conclusion of both a poem and a life, especially of a life ending amid political turmoil. The Irish materials in canto VI point to a date no earlier than 1586, since before he had installed himself in his Kilcolman estate Spenser would probably not have known in detail the area near Arlo-hill. And Cynthia's (Elizabeth's) abandonment of it to wolves and thieves (7.6.55) seems a tactful reference to the rout of the English during Tyrone's rebellion, which began early in June of 1598. Finally, Spenser had already told the Bregog and Mulla story in 'Colin Clouts Come Home Againe', probably not written before 1591, and he alludes to it in 6.36.40 of *Mutabilitie*. All this suggests a late date of composition, probably between the autumn of 1598 and Spenser's death on 13 January of the following year.

Since sentimental interest attaches to assigning the *Cantos* as late a date as possible, some have resisted it on stylistic or other grounds. Spenser's style does not develop through well-marked periods, however, and some attempts to wrest the date of the *Cantos* from their style have led to equivocal answers. Yet Padelford states that:

> The feminine endings prove that the *Cantos of Mutabilitie* must have been written after the first three books. The compound words and run-over lines would suggest that they were composed before Book VI. The far weightier evidence, however, of certain distinctive peculiarities of composition favours a date subsequent even to *The Legend of Courtesie*.[1]

One concludes that the version of the *Cantos* we now have was almost certainly his last effort on *The Faerie Queene*.

None of this should rule out the possibility that Spenser had conceived the outline for something like the *Cantos* some years earlier. After Mrs Bennett's exposition in *The Evolution of the Faerie Queene* (1942), we cannot put much stock in the notion of *seriatim* composition. And thematic connections between the *Cantos* and Spenser's earlier work, as well as the consummate artistry of the piece, compel us to allow that Spenser may

[1] F. M. Padelford, '*The Cantos of Mutabilitie*: Further Considerations Bearing on the Date', *PMLA* 45 (1940), 711.

have turned to perfect materials he had toyed with, or even sketched out, before.

THE BACKGROUND OF THE *CANTOS*

The Faerie Queene is so various and huge, the *Cantos* so extensive in their implications, that to place them in a literary or even cultural 'setting' is almost to reason in a circle. Despite what has been called their 'medievalism', they seem to define and gather up their age. Specifically, the *Cantos* disclose much of the philosophic and political outlook and of the aims and conditions of authorship dominant during the later 1500s. The qualifying word 'dominant' is necessary, for society and letters were altering rapidly toward the turn of the century, and *The Faerie Queene*, like most epics, is a work of retrospection, if not nostalgia. One must also remember that most Elizabethans left behind annals shorter and simpler than *The Faerie Queene*.

In particular, the *Cantos* exhibit what Tillyard and others have popularized as the 'Elizabethan World Picture'; a benign Creator, a Creation whose plenitude exhausted possibility, this plenitude ordered in hierarchies and analogies of being —then the grand design thrown into confusion by the Fall, with the divine original veiled behind the mutability of a fallen world and a corresponding disorder in human faculties, which now only Grace could alleviate. The *Cantos* give us nearly the whole of this. Elizabethan and older cosmologies are suffused through the poem, in its fable as well as in such details as the positions of the planet deities, the conception of the four elements, and the description of Nature's assembly. Mutabilitie herself is a condition and consequence of the Fall; the inability of her 'aspiring mind' (here recall Marlowe's theme in *Faustus*), to understand its own contradictions in the pageant argument yet another consequence. The Irish digression applies the theme of order to the political realm. Nature's judgment, and the movement toward redemption implicit in the pageant of the months and in the fate of Molanna, suggest Grace and the ultimate perfection to which the concluding stanzas appeal. In sum, the *Cantos* are a testament to the optimism of earlier Renaissance Anglicanism.

On the historical side, Elizabethan nationalism and the cult of Elizabeth herself colour both the major action and the Faunus digression, hence the central rôle of Cynthia-Diana in both. On the literary side, the poet's striving for Fame (see 6.7.1–2) is an extension of this nationalist spirit. And the (to our day) unfortunate overtones of imperialism and ambition are somewhat relieved (or perhaps worsened) by association with 'heavenly things', for both poets and nations were thought to be engaged in an effort to achieve something paralleling and worthy of the divine order.

In detail, the *Cantos* reflect the intellectual and stylistic eclecticism of the time, gathering up many of its leading concerns and techniques: quasi-Platonic idealism, the logic and rhetoric of the schools, the emblematic expression and didactic aims of Elizabethan verse. Classical or medieval debate and allegory, pageant and exemplum, are suffused with Ovidian sensuousness and controlled by a narrative form developed from Italian example.

But by the later 1590s such an achievement, though grand, was becoming old-fashioned. The *Cantos* preserve a literary and intellectual stance that had become difficult as the *primavera* quality of literature in the earlier years of Elizabeth's reign darkened into religious doubt and mannerist style. Before the *Cantos* were published, *Troilus and Cressida* and *Hamlet* were on the boards. Donne was already well along in the composition of a new poetry which cleared away the 'dull pedantique weeds' of classical myth, altered the macrocosmic (universe-to-man) analogy to portray, not universal harmony, but upset subjective states, and toyed with literary decorum to achieve satire and surprise.

RELATION OF THE *CANTOS* TO THE REST OF *THE FAERIE QUEENE*

The stanza form and summary proems, the division into cantos (though this may not be Spenser's), the allusions to epic decorum in 7.6.37 and to Faery Land in 7.6.2.4—these, together with their style and matter, relate the *Mutabilitie Cantos* to the rest of *The Faerie Queene*. But narrative discontinuities in Books I–VI, and the obvious integrity of the *Cantos* themselves, have made their relations to the rest of the epic a subject of controversy. In earlier discussion, there are attempts to place the *Cantos* in some hypothetical plan or sequence of composition. In later there is a tacit acceptance of the folio order as a given, and a search for some esthetic pattern to account for its success.

In early commentary the *Cantos* were presented as a separate poem (Sebastian Evans), or a portion of a second epic (Thomas Wise), as possibly attached to Books II, III, or V (William DeMoss), or as early sketches, rejected on Harvey's advice, then salvaged for sections of Books III and V (Evelyn Albright).[1] The value of such discussions lies in their identification of recurring themes and nuances. But the fallacy of totally 'planned' composition is especially inapplicable to *The Faerie Queene*. Spenser's letter to Raleigh, 'A Letter of the Authors expounding his whole intention in the course of this worke', ought to cool almost at once the hopes its rubric encourages, for in it Spenser described the beginning of Sir Guyon's quest in a manner contradicted by the text he was introducing.

In the last two decades, scholars have left the poet's workshop for his text. Their conclusions seem to be that Spenser was probably uninterested in consistent sequential fable, and that his particular innovation in construction lay in 'the self-contained character of each book (except for III and IV which partly run together)'.[2] In its large structural features, *The Faerie Queene* seems to stand between more linear Italian epics and a mosaic like *The Canterbury Tales*. The most fruitful inquiries into the relations of the parts of *The Faerie Queene* treat accumulating theme and parallel tone or literary strategy

[1] This phase of the discussion has been skilfully tracked in the *Variorum* VI, Appendix 2.

[2] G. Hough, *Preface to The Faerie Queene* (1962), p. 225.

rather than strict narrative sequence or connection through superficial narrative strands such as the structurally unimportant quest of Arthur for Gloriana.

Among the more obvious thematic antecedents of the *Cantos* are the Garden of Adonis episode, the prologue to Book V, and the dispute between Artegall and the extremist Giant. Other relations are less obvious. Episodes in *The Faerie Queene* are embodiments of recurring states of feeling. If the Bower of Bliss reifies sensual temptation, the *Mutabilitie Cantos* give us something more complex and rare: the Christian's qualified delight in a world both wondrous and fallen. Thus, like other parts of *The Faerie Queene*, the *Cantos* unfold an attitude. Further, they represent—as do the House of Holiness and the Garden of Adonis—what C. S. Lewis called an 'allegorical core' or 'shrine or inner stage' in which the central theme of a whole book of the epic is clearly realized amid the 'pathless wandering' of 'a loose fringe of stories'. And the imagery of the *Cantos*, embracing four levels of existence: death and corruption, ordinary experience, uncorrupted nature, and God, not only relates them to the rest of *The Faerie Queene*, but seems a coda to the whole.[1]

Inevitably, such observations on technique shade into discussions of themes. The 'philosophy' of the *Cantos*—to give their thought a name poetry rarely aspires to and never earns— are best treated apart. Yet it is relevant at the outset to ask if the *Cantos* are a rejection of earlier attitudes in *The Faerie Queene* or a compatible if not wholly consistent development of them.

Recent opinion favours the latter position. D. C. Allen states a prevailing view when he finds Renaissance thought 'a philosophic nightmare' in which Spenser and his contemporaries groped toward eclectic harmonies rather than logical system. But though he concludes that Nature's verdict 'does not arise from the logic of the piece', and that the thought of the *Cantos*

[1] Northrop Frye, 'The Structure of Imagery in *The Faerie Queene*', *UTQ* 30 (1961), 109–27.

is 'a sort of *tour de force*', he yet sees in the *Cantos* a resolution of the poet's doubts.[1]

Those whose religious outlook is closer to Spenser's have put the case more sympathetically. For C. S. Lewis the *Cantos* present an instance of 'Spenser's last-moment withdrawal from dualism', from the situation of those figures in medieval literature (Chaucer's Troilus is one) who throw their hearts to the world and painfully retrieve them in a palinode. In any case, the *Cantos* are not a philosophic reversal, but part of a harmony that encompasses the entire *Faerie Queene*.

Others have elaborated this view. Graham Hough, for example, speaks of the 'organic growth' of the *Faerie Queene* through related themes, and observes that 'if Spenser is the great poet of natural happiness, he also knows its limits and its lack'. Both the happiness and the limits are present in the *Cantos* as elsewhere; only the emphasis is altered.

Yet there are significant differences between the *Cantos* and the rest of *The Faerie Queene*. Elsewhere in Spenser's mythological digressions, there is no dramatic action, and agents from the narrative bind digression to plot. Elsewhere in the epic's narrative sections, human or demi-human agents operate within the framework of chivalry. But in the *Cantos* there is a dramatic confrontation, and gods and abstractions contend in a cosmic and philosophic framework. Stampfer attributes these differences to 'a sense of the ultimate futility of human action in regard to the general structure of the universe' that darkens as *The Faerie Queene* progresses.[2] Book I, he observes, ends with a dragon slain; Book II with Acrasia bound, but still alive; Book V with Artegall withdrawing, his mission incomplete. In Book VI Stampfer finds the 'breakdown of the allegory' complete. This growing sense of futility, he contends, coupled

---

[1] D. C. Allen, 'The Degeneration of Man and Renaissance Pessimism', *SP* 35 (1938), 206, 208.

[2] J. L. Stampfer, '*The Cantos of Mutabilitie*: Spenser's Last Testament of Faith', *UTQ* 21 (1952), 141–4.

with the Irish catastrophe, led Spenser to abandon 'the whole chivalric tissue of knights and ladies' and the 'leisurely' purpose of fashioning a gentleman, and to write the *Mutabilitie Cantos* as a more direct confrontation of 'deeper problems of existence'. Yet Acrasia's death would have been illogical (entailing Sir Guyon's death as well, the death of Temperance), since the temptation Acrasia represents is a permanent fact of the earthly condition. Moreover, the 'sense of the ultimate futility of human action' in regard to the general structure of the universe is a tenet, not a dismaying discovery, of Christian orthodoxy; hence Artegall's case is not unpredictable. As early as 'The Ruines of Time' Spenser wrote that 'deeds do die, how euer noblie donne'.

Perhaps one ought to see the *Cantos* as the height of a climb rather than the turning of a corner. There is, in fact, in the *Cantos* an imagined person, acting within the frame of chivalry, linking the *Cantos* to the rest of the poem. This character is the narrator himself, who emerges in the opening lines, in the humour of the council of the gods, in the wry references to the Irish situation, in the concluding prayer. Perhaps one ought to view the *Cantos* as the final development of this character toward an exemplification of the Christian gentleman the epic was intended to form. What one sees then is neither morbidity nor pessimistic revision, but a dramatic instance of holy living, with its delight and concern for the proper use of nature, and holy dying, with its calm recognition of what is abandoned and what is to be gained. Spenser's vision here, as Millar Maclure observed, 'is the ultimate vision . . . the "Sabaoths sight" to which the poet himself looks forward, and of which his *art* in its highest reaches is a mysterious type and symbol'.[1] The final stanzas of *The Faerie Queene* seem to divest themselves of a concern with the contingent and to give us, as at the outset of the epic, an isolated figure, but one questing toward a different end. They complete the action of the epic by presenting a transcendence implied in the orthodox insistence on the

[1] M. Maclure, 'Nature and Art in *The Faerie Queene*', *ELH* 28 (1961), 20.

2

value of both mutable nature and divine Grace. This movement from the even-toned narrator of the first to the passionate suppliant of the last stanza is perhaps the most useful context for an initial view of the *Cantos*.

AN APPROACH TO THE *CANTOS*:

THEIR SPIRIT

Of Elizabethan literary commonplaces, temporal change or mutability was the most common. Possibly the theme of love seems more pervasive, but protestations to one's mistress and protests against her were equally protests against Time. One loved 'in Time's despite', and one lost to 'newfanglenesse'. Thus the title *Cantos of Mutabilitie* might lead us to expect yet another lament over 'bare ruined choirs where late the sweet birds sang'. And if one were to scan only the first stanza of canto VI, with its reference to Mutabilitie's 'cruell sports', and the first of canto VIII, with its expression of loathing 'for this state of life so tickle', one would think the expectation fulfilled.

Certainly Spenser knew the tune by heart, having tried it from his apprentice days. But when (translating Tasso almost literally) he sings it most exquisitely, as in:

> So passeth, in the passing of a day,
> Of mortall life, the leafe, the bud, the flowre,

he puts it in the mouth of a minion of Acrasia, the nympho-maniac witch of the Bower of Bliss (2.12.75). Or he makes the 'still chaunging state' of man the burden of Despair's tempta-tion of the Red-crosse Knight (1.9.39ff.). In both cases, Spenser is concerned that we see how sorrowing over mutability may screen self-indulgence.

So the *Mutabilitie Cantos* are both surprising and inevitable in their spirit of almost continuous gaiety. The pageant of the seasons, a command parade in poems on earthly transience, is here. But not even the year's end is funereal. Winter enters the celestial courtroom on a pun, 'cloathed all in frize'. And he is not the dread instrument of malign Nature, but a comical wretch, chattering and purple-billed. Before he has shambled by it is we who must pity him, 'for he was faint with cold and weak with eld'.

Mutabilitie herself is less menace than ingenue. Her boldness is made attractive, and there is a pretty contretemps when she elbows into Heaven. Starry divinities stand about 'all astonied, like a sort of Steeres', and even Jove on his throne 'gan straight dispose / Himself more full of grace and Majestie'. Jove is not only put on his dignity, he has an eye for the lady, who is 'as beautiful of face / As any of the goddesses in place'. After a burst of rage and a taking-up of thunderbolts, Jove hesitates. Moreover, on the question of legitimate succession to power, the lady has a point: hers may not be a good family, but it is surely an old one.

The *Cantos* are also free of that martial 'sternenesse of stile' which the poet, having things both ways, finds it ill-fitting to abandon for 'soft delights' (6.37). He feels free to ask Clio (the muse of history) to lend her pen to Calliope (the muse of heroic verse). And even without such polite invocation, he seems to tax Thalia (the muse of comic and pastoral verse) for aid as well. The *Cantos* are redolent of stream and brake; they digress to foolish fauns. A *joie de vivre* insinuates itself into the philosophic matter. And in the manliness of the concluding prayer, rest 'Vpon the pillours of Eternity' is not a hermetic rejection, but a Christian acceptance of the common fate, appropriate to the fullest life. Nor does Spenser try to have things both ways here. The apparent embrace and rejection of temporal experience in the *Cantos* are not the old double pull to relish the world and to despise it. It is precisely this dualism which Spenser escapes. For him the world seems to be good as means, bad as end. The *Cantos* are an attempt at eschatology, a statement about last things.

THEIR ORGANIZATION

The poem is made up of three movements, two of them narrative, one intellectual. The two narrative movements are

Mutabilitie's attempt to usurp Jove's power, and Faunus' attempt to violate Cynthia's modesty. The Faunus incident is pastoral and comic, a below-stairs counterpart of the more serious, heroic incursion of Mutabilitie; Faunus' desire to see Cynthia divested is analogous to Mutabilitie's desire to divest her of power.

In both cases, Cynthia is the immediate object of attack. As the Moon, she governs lawfully the sphere of Mutabilitie's *de facto* power. For Mutabilitie to displace Cynthia, then, is for her to declare war on universal order. But Cynthia is also 'soueraine Queene profest / Of woods and forrests', especially those of Arlo-hill, a favourite mountain near Kilcolman Castle, Spenser's Irish home. For Faunus to corrupt her servants and violate her privacy is for him to outrage universal order's social miniature.

The rôles of Cynthia in both incidents are consistent with Spenser's use of her as a surrogate for Queen Elizabeth. The Queen's spinsterhood had suggested the identification to many poets. Spenser refers to Sir Walter Raleigh's poem, the *Book of the Ocean to Cynthia* (most of it now lost), in stanzas 4 and 5 of the introduction to Book III of *The Faerie Queene*. In his letter to Raleigh, Spenser remarks of Elizabeth that 'she beareth two persons, the one of a most royall Queene or Empresse', the other of a most 'vertuous and beautifull Lady', and that he intends to represent her according to Raleigh's 'excellent conceipt of Cynthia (Phoebe and Cynthia being names for Diana)'. It is the 'royall Empresse' whom Mutabilitie would displace, the 'vertuous and beautifull Lady' at whom Faunus would peep.

From the Irish and royal references we may conclude that the Faunus incident has a political meaning; moreover, Spenser prefaces it with an invocation of the muse of history. Specifically, it is an interpolated anecdote serving as an example of how Mutabilitie's revolt in heaven is paralleled on earth. It relates to Mutabilitie's assault somewhat as do the Falstaff scenes to the major conspiracy in *Henry IV, part 1*, as a diminishing of the seriousness of the Mutabilitie incident, and thus also as a foreshadowing of the unsuccessful outcome of Mutabilitie's appeal to Nature. Cynthia's decision not to kill or geld Faunus, rather to leave Arlo-hill to its wolves and bandits, parallels Nature's decision which, though it goes against Mutabilitie, bids her continue ruling over temporal affairs.

Both incidents prepare for the concluding stanzas. The prayer to the Sabbaoth God is less significant without these divine decisions that wolves must go on ravaging the lovely hill, and Mutabilitie go on reigning beneath the moon—at least until things 'work their owne perfection'.

But the function of these narrative movements is not merely that of foreshadowing the prayer, which concludes the intellectual movement of the poem. The attacks on Cynthia afford Spenser the opportunity to work out the evolution of the narrator. To understand this evolution, one must understand its goal.

The concluding prayer is not simply a 'Come, Sweet Death', that follows personal loss and the *contemptus mundi*. In the parade of Mutabilitie's allegorical witnesses, Death is 'most grim and griesly', yet 'but a parting of the breath', and 'vnsoul'd' as well as 'unbodied'. Death is a fact of nature, not an object of desire. Life, not only the 'faire young lusty boy' of the pageant, but life in all its forms, in the thickets of Arlo-hill, in the councils of the gods, is desired and valued. The language of the poem prompts this conclusion, for in the *Cantos*, no less than in Elizabethan drama, expression is a distillation of character. And the evolution of the narrator is defined by his expression of the delights and limitations of temporality.

Taken together, these narrative and intellectual movements give us the orthodox Anglican moral vision, not only the substance of the vision, but, in the development of the narrator, the sensibility that the vision demands. To label this vision and sensibility rejections of the world is a simplification. Precisely how they differ from so-called 'medieval' palinode and puritan rejection is best treated after the narrative itself has been examined more closely.

THE NARRATIVES

a. Mutabilitie's Attack on Order: the Major Narrative

The major narrative of the *Cantos* begins with Mutabilitie's desire to be recognized as a goddess, and to extend her sway over the heavens (1–4), displacing Jove. She enters the Circle of the Moon, and bids Cynthia relinquish her throne (7–13). The heavens fear the return of primal Chaos, and Mercury runs in alarm to Jove (13–15), who sends him to deter Mutabilitie (16–17). But she is immune to his mace (18), and Mercury returns to Jove, who has by now assembled the gods (19). Taking advantage of their dismay, Mutabilitie enters their council (24), and despite her initial awe, asserts her lineage as justification of her claim to Jove's position (26–27). The gods are impressed, and Jove, after rebuking her rebellion (28–30), is moved by her beauty to extenuate it (31–32). But Mutabilitie refuses to abandon her claim, and appeals beyond Jove to the God of Nature (33–35). Grudgingly, Jove agrees to have the case decided on Arlo-hill (36).

The major narrative resumes in canto VII before an assembly of all Creation, over which Dame Nature, mysterious and indescribable (5–9), presides as judge. Mutabilitie begins her case, arguing that Jove has powers that are hers by inheritance and position (14–19). She, rather than the gods, controls the 'groundwork' of the world, the elements of Earth, Water, Air, and Fire (17–25). She then asks Nature to permit the calling of witnesses (27). The Seasons (28–31), the Months (32–43), Day, Night, and the Hours, and Life and Death (44–46) appear to testify to her power, though their testimony actually implies the opposite. Jove concedes Mutabilitie's sublunary rule, but argues that the gods, controlling Time, and thus dictating change, are superior to Mutabilitie (48). She counters that these powers are not demonstrable (49), that the gods themselves are subject to change, not excluding Jove (50–53), and that their varying courses in the heavens are proof of her assertion (54–55). She concludes by once again appealing to Nature (56). At last Nature declares that all things are indeed subject to alteration, but that alteration involves no change of their essence, only an unfolding of their potentialities. Through this unfolding, things perfect themselves, returning always to their initial, divinely intended natures. Hence, they triumph over change, not change over them (58). She concludes by urging Mutabilitie's submission, and the Titaness is silenced. Her judgment given, Nature suddenly vanishes (59).

This is the most decorous of rebellions. After the interruption of Jove's council, Mutabilitie's rebellion becomes a law-suit, with both parties tacitly agreed on observing the decencies. And after the early suggestions of its similarity to the fall of Lucifer and 'man's first disobedience', the tragic implications of the rebellion are allowed to fade. These peculiarities of tale and telling may be understood somewhat better if we determine who Mutabilitie is and just what she wants.

The lineage Spenser provides for Mutabilitie defines her claim and something of her character. Mutabilitie descends from the Titans, the children of Heaven and Earth, who deposed their father, setting one of their number, Time (Saturn or Cronus), on his throne. Saturn was in turn overthrown by his son Jove, who expelled the Titans from heaven, though he allowed many of their descendants considerable power. If Mutabilitie is of 'that bad seed' of Titans and rebels, so is Jove. So also is Cynthia, for with Hecate she shares in a triple identity (cf. Ovid, *Metamorphoses* 7.94; 'triple Hecate', in *Midsummer Night's Dream* and Keats' sonnet 'To Homer'), the other sharer being Luna (cf. Virgil, *Aeneid* 6.247). Jove could, of course, claim that his rebellion was directed against a usurper. But this would involve an appeal to some anterior legitimizing Power. Perhaps one may see the hand of such a Power in Jove's lucky survival despite Saturn's agreement with Titan. Evidently Mutabilitie thinks not, as may be seen from her telling of the 'Corybantes' slight'. Saturn's elder brother had agreed to allow Saturn rule over heaven provided he destroyed his children, thus leaving no successor. But his wife Rhea concealed Jove's birth-cries in the noise made by the Corybantes, her attendants, who loudly beat their shields. This is the 'slight' or trick of 6.27. As Sawtelle points out, Spenser found this version of the myth in the handbook of mythology by Comes. Mutabilitie uses it to emphasize the legitimacy of her claim as a descendant of Titan; for this purpose it is preferable to the more common version (found in Hesiod), which emphasizes the rebellion of the Titans against their father, and Jove's victory in open combat.[1] In any case, the jostling for divinity in the *Cantos* is a family squabble, and Mutabilitie's claim to succession not wholly unfounded. At best, Jove can claim orthodoxy, but he cannot claim to be its source. The genealogies of Jove and Mutabilitie demonstrate that the issue between them is not a matter of genealogy at all. Indeed, no one but Mutabilitie actually takes the view that it is. The issue is one of their relation to higher powers, to Nature, and to a Power higher still, whom Spenser contrives to omit from the narrative entirely.

We must conclude, then, that the divinities of the *Cantos*, Jove included, are clearly of God, but not to be identified with Him. He is not to be tried. The gods of the *Cantos* are planetary deities, and as such, the symbols of natural laws, or of their administration. On this view, Mutabilitie's status becomes clearer. She is a process claiming to be a law, an agent desiring to be a principal.

It can be argued that these distinctions between law and process are not strictly preserved. The gods, as planetary deities, alter in their courses, and Mutabilitie is prompt to call this to the attention of the bench. There was no denying her the argument; it was a commonplace. Not until Kepler's work on elliptical orbits (1609), could the notion of erratic planetary movement, based on the primitive assumptions of circular orbits, begin to be dispelled. Spenser himself had spoken of

---

[1] A. A. Sawtelle, *Sources of Spenser's Classical Mythology* (1896), pp. 115–6; see also Osgood, *Variorum* VI, p. 279, on the language of the passage and its resemblance to Comes' 'simulatis sacrificiis'.

the wandering of the planets since the Golden Age as por-
tending 'the world's last ruinous decay'. It was too good a
point for the plaintiff to be omitted.

Yet one must not see this as an earlier version of the radical
consternation aroused later by the 'new astronomy'. Spenser
seems not to have been interested in scientific discoveries. He
is echoing two old traditions: that at the Fall a shock disordered
Creation, and that the earth was subject to decay. These ideas
—though undoubtedly fostering a sense of loss—did not always
lead to pessimism. D. C. Allen writes, with a touch of irony,
that 'One does not ponder the deterioration from older forms
and then adopt the perfectionist's creed without a minor
premise'.[1] For Spenser the 'minor premise' was Anglican
Christianity, which offered the hope of a millenial perfection.

If in the *Cantos* Spenser seems reluctant to explore ultimate
mysteries directly, more reluctant for example than Milton,
who brings God into his cast of characters, his veil of allegory
is no sign of imperfect faith. It is, in fact, a more 'religious'
strategy than Milton's (the idea is C. S. Lewis's), suggesting
the primal taboos against naming and summoning. And it is a
better literary strategy. Perfection is a dull subject.

But Spenser had no reason to mention God directly before
canto VIII. The *Cantos* were part of a Legend of Constancie
which would elucidate that virtue. Mutabilitie's revolt would
call the virtue of constancy into question by attempting to
show it as inoperative in a fallen world. Her revolt, however, is
not to be regarded as directly an attack on God. He is not
assailed, nor is Nature, to whom Mutabilitie both appeals and
submits. What Mutabilitie wants is actually a change at the
under-secretarial level of bureaucracy, not an overthrow of
government. Had the latter been the case, there would be
stronger grounds for Greenlaw's idea that the *Cantos* present
a variety of Lucretian naturalism. As it is, Mutabilitie's
limited ambitions permit a mock-heroic air, an absence of
narrative tension, a relaxed opulence of rhetoric and pageant,
an easy accommodation of the Faunus episode and, above all,

[1] D. C. Allen, *loc. cit.*, 218.

a sympathetic presentation of Mutabilitie herself, an ambitious girl of good spirit who comes round in the end.

Mutabilitie's self-restraint forestalls the tragic theme we expect in works that treat revolt against Law and revolt in Heaven. Rosemond Tuve remarks that the *Cantos* are the 'earliest important attempt to state seriously in poetry the accusations later so common in *libertin* thought'.[1] But the force of these accusations is wholly directed at Spenser's mythological figures. The decisive moment in the narrative comes in canto VI.35, when Mutabilitie says:

> to the highest him, that is behight
> Father of Gods and men by equall might;
> To weet, the God of Nature, I appeale.

With this, it becomes clear the rebellion will be contained. Appropriately Spenser then begins the delightful sub-plot.

Before the appeal 'to the highest him', there was perhaps reason to be concerned. The record of Mutabilitie's reign beneath the moon was full of 'sad examples'. She had perverted the 'good estate' of things, broken the laws of Justice and Policy, made bad of good, exchanged life for death. In the penultimate phrase she resembles Lucifer ('Evil be thou my good'), and in the last, disobedient Adam. But though these transgressions occurred during her reign, Mutabilitie is more an effect of them than a cause. It was the Fall of Man that set off mutability by bringing 'Death into the world and all our woe', not Mutabilitie who caused the Fall. History is Mutabilitie's record, and 'the appeal to History', as Cardinal Manning observed, 'is a sin against the Holy Spirit'. Spenser was too orthodox to be guilty of it. A contrary view, that 'Spenser practically identifies his Titaness with sin' and corruption is urged by C. S. Lewis.[2] But if Mutabilitie can be charged with old age, death, and the Fall, she also causes changes that are both innocent and desirable.

[1] Rosemond Tuve, *Elizabethan and Metaphysical Imagery* (1947), p. 207.
[2] *Allegory of Love*, pp. 353ff.

The accusations against Mutabilitie in canto VI.4–6 should probably be thought of as something like an extended metonymy 'where the adjoint is put for the thing to which it is adjoyned. . . . So in the Epistle to the Ephesians: *The dayes are evil, that is, the manner conversation, and the deeds of men in the dayes*'. Or, on a slightly different view of Mutabilitie's relation to evil, as a metonymy 'where the thing caused or the effect is put for any of [its] causes'.[1] Spenser's readers would have understood the figure and the possibility that it concealed a flaw in logic. The inevitable question is why Spenser would have chosen to encourage what is in effect a misleading accusation against Mutabilitie. She herself is not evil; as Sister M. Pauline Parker states she is 'not a moral figure at all', but 'a natural force'.[2]

It will not do to say simply that introducing Mutabilitie as *femme fatale* arouses dire expectation, though this is the case. If it were Spenser's only reason we should be justified in sniffing red herring. The unfair metonymy is rather the confusion about Mutabilitie that the *Cantos* attempt to clarify. Spenser seems to encourage it at the outset so that his readers, coming at last to Nature's judgment, may see precisely where they have been led. The charges against Mutabilitie are Despair's argument and Acrasia's excuse; they erroneously transfer the guilt of Man to the temporal condition. Spenser had made the point before. But any Legend of Constancie would have had to make it again, lest Constancie be misdefined by reference to its apparent opposite, merely temporal change. So the *Cantos* begin with the position they refute, embodying it in a passage which suggests the logical defect of the position.

If this helps to clarify the meaning of Mutabilitie and her part of the narrative, it also clarifies the development of the narrator. *The Faerie Queene* is a didactic poem, and teaching presumes an ignorance to be dispelled. The narrator acts, in

[1] The citations are from Dudley Fenner, *The Artes of Logike and Rhetorike* (1584), sig. Dir, quoted in Sister Miriam Joseph, *Shakespeare's Use of the Arts of Language* (1947), pp. 320, 336.

[2] Sister M. Pauline Parker, *Allegory of the Faerie Queene* (1960), p. 263.

the *Cantos* at least, as the reader's surrogate in this process, his accusations against Mutabilitie giving way to another point of view. If this seems contrary to Spenser's practice elsewhere we must remember that, in the cosmic setting of the *Cantos*, the narrator stands for questing Everyman. In the final prayer, the *Cantos* spiral back over the materials of their beginning. But the prayer differs from the earlier accusations against temporal change. The rejection of 'this state of life so tickle' is not made because change is evil, but because mutability—sad or delightful—is merely a process, inferior to the state that will be revealed at 'the great Sabaoth's sight'.

The goal dignifies the process. Mutabilitie, for all her limitations, has undeniable rights and powers. Citing the *Fowre Hymnes* as a source for Spenser's views on beauty, Sister M. Pauline Parker argues that if 'Mutabilitie's beauty be great and real, there is good in her'. The view is corroborated by Mutabilitie's vitality and strength, her immunity to Hermes' staff, the deference shown her by Jove, and Nature's patience with her case.[1] The justification for Spenser's positive representation of Mutabilitie is to be found in Nature's judgment of her case. Through her, men

> their being doe dilate
> And turning to themselves at length againe,
> Do worke their owne perfection. . . .

Mutabilitie is not only a way out of Eden but a way back. Change is not random or erratic, but directed by the desire of all things to realize their particular perfections.

For all this she can be cruel, foolish, and haughty. Jove compares her to a host of rebels against law and heaven. But this is before he actually looks at her. There is something amusing in this apparent ignorance in Spenser's mythological figures of one another's functions. Perhaps administrative redundance is the difficulty of any bureaucracy, even a pantheon. And Spenser is aware of these comic overtones,

[1] *Loc. cit.*; cf. Hough *op. cit.*, 165, for another view of Spenser's attitude toward beauty.

exploiting them in Jove's self-conscious, 'But ah' (6.31), when he reminds himself that he is, after all, a god. But Mutabilitie's place in the cosmic system is clear. If she is variously praised and condemned it is because, like any process, she is a good servant but a bad master.

Interpretations of allegorical narrative are also good servants and bad masters. However tactful or informed, they mangle one detail or miss another. This is as it ought to be. Were it not so, recent strictures against allegory would be just: it would provide only pretty jumbles of what had been better said straight.

b. Faunus and Diana: the Minor Narrative

The tale of Faunus is Ovidian, based on the Actaeon and Diana myth in the *Metamorphoses*. The story was widely used. In the Duke's opening speech in *Twelfth Night* the Actaeon story is alluded to as a parable of uncontrolled passion. In Golding's 'Epistle' to his translation of Ovid (ll.97ff.), it is a warning to those who spend their time 'in foule excesse of chamberworke, or too much meate and drink'. For Abraham Fraunce it illustrated the danger of prying into those matters, 'which be above our reache'.[1] To Spenser there would have been no incompatibility among these interpretations; in *The Faerie Queene* a central mystery of nature is the generative function. Overtones of all these Elizabethan uses of the Actaeon story are present in the Faunus episode. In it Spenser treats of Faunus' bribery of Molanna, who aids him to spy on her mistress Diana; of his laughter at the chaste goddess' nakedness; of his subsequent punishment and of Diana's abandonment of Arlo-hill and Ireland. But again, as in the case of Mutabilitie's revolt, the tragic and ironic possibilities of the story are carefully attenuated. Faunus is ridiculous rather than pitiful, as is Actaeon. Unlike Actaeon he is not changed into a stag, merely clad in deerskin. The nymphs hunt him with their own hounds, not with his. Finally, he is only

---

[1] Abraham Fraunce, *The Third Part of the Countess of Pembrokes Yuychurch* (1592), p. 43.

exhausted in the chase, not set on and torn to pieces. Molanna's punishment too is mitigated in a pretty conceit. She is stoned, but with the result that she becomes even more shallow a stream. And Faunus' promise to her is fulfilled when she joins her beloved Fanchin.

As with the main narrative, there are obvious parallels to the story of the Fall. Arlo-hill is a kind of Eden, 'the best and fairest . . . in all this holy-Islands hights'. Molanna, who ought to have been obedient to her mistress, is tempted by a half-animal deity, first with flattering words, then with 'Queene-apples and cherries'. And, as after the Fall, Arlo-hill becomes a prey to vicissitude and evil. But the biblical allusions do not harden into the tragic implications of the Fall. Faunus is no Satan, but a foolish faun. The tempting queene-apples and cherries are as much a reminder of pastoral verse, or of the lover's gift pippins in the *Art of Love*, as of the fatal apple of *Genesis*. Arlo-hill is not a paradise to which one cannot return; it is Irish, beautiful still, 'the richest champian that may else be rid'; it is peopled by 'in-dwellers' and by the 'Wood-gods breed'. Moreover, Arlo-hill becomes in canto VII a symbol of harmony restored, for it is the scene of Diana's vindication by Nature, and of the orderly assemblage of all creation. But equally important in restraining the tragic possibilities of the story is the intervention of the narrator in tone and detail. For example, Faunus is condescendingly parenthesized as a 'poore soule', and Diana's concern for her modesty amusingly compared in mock-epic simile to the care of 'an hus-wife' who 'Thinks of her Dairie to make wondrous gaine'.

For all this, the episode is not simply light-hearted digression; it relates to the main narrative and serves as political allegory, though the security of Spenser's philosophic position frees him for a levity in conception and detail.

Relations to the main narrative are numerous. Both Faunus' intrusion and Mutabilitie's revolt are attempts on Cynthia and order; both are resolved with judgments that rebuke but do not destroy the offenders. Both Faunus and Mutabilitie are perdurable: the wood-god's breed may not be spilled;

Mutabilitie must govern beneath the moon until the close of human time. Both are prankish, impulsive, even outrageous—though Mutabilitie suggests something closer to the ultimately corrupt than does her less serious counterpart. This is because Mutabilitie has a philosophic abstractness that puts her beyond human reach, while Faunus is sensuality, what leads to mutability in individual man, and thus, though ineradicable, more readily subject to chastisement. Just as significant structurally, however, is Spenser's use of the Faunus episode to foreshadow the outcome of Mutabilitie's revolt, and thus relieve its apparent seriousness. In addition, the episode functions thematically by foreshadowing the hidden meaning of the pageant and of the judgment of Nature. In Molanna's 'reward', her joining with her beloved Fanchin, there is something of the *felix culpa* implied in Nature's explanation of change. And the myth of Alpheus and Arethusa, which their story resembles, was allegorized in at least one source Spenser knew (Comes 6.24), as the desire of imperfection for virtue. If the continuance of the wood-god's breed suggests divine forbearance after the Fall, Diana's 'heavy haplesse curse' suggests God's wrath. Out of such suggestions, as out of Nature's judgment, emerges the idea of a tangible world in process, both ravaged and beautiful, groping to return to its original state. What Spenser is depicting in the Faunus episode is not so much the loss of Eden itself as the less momentous echoes of that event—where sin appears as the attrition of the everyday, and good seems to emerge as a casual by-product.

It was not inconvenient for Spenser to treat the Faunus narrative as political allegory. The landscape is Irish, History the aiding muse, and Diana Elizabeth. 'That lands in-dwellers', Spenser among them, found its reputation for wolves and thieves only 'too-too true' at the time the *Cantos* were written. The topographical details indicate the care Spenser exercised in making the setting unmistakable. A recent attempt by Stampfer[1] to connect the Faunus episode with Irish politics

[1] J. L. Stampfer, *loc. cit.*, 152ff.

identifies Faunus with the Irish rebel (or patriot) Tyrone who corrupted Molanna (the Irish populace, and hence Diana's maid) with queene-apples (sovereignty) and cherries (the promise of the free practice of Roman Catholicism), and the promise of a union with Fanchin (either the Church, which dispensed the waters of grace, or political freedom). Faunus' frequent viewing of Diana clothed is taken to refer to Tyrone's stay in England or his exercise of limited sovereignty over Donegal; and Faunus' foolish laughter, to Tyrone's inability to restrain his desires as evidenced politically by his assumption in 1595 of the designation of the ancient Irish kings. The difficulty of Diana's nymphs in deciding what to do with Faunus is thought to resemble Elizabethan indecision over Irish policy. Diana's forsaking of Ireland is taken as a tactful allusion to the initial English military defeats, and the changes Spenser made in Ovid's stories of Actaeon and Arethusa as also explicable on the grounds of political allegory. Though generally plausible, this version of the political allegory suffers from both vagueness and arbitrary specificity. The temptation with queene-apples may be read with equal validity as the pastoral love-convention of the gift of fruit which runs from Theocritus through Virgil (*Eclogues* 2.51), from whom Spenser picks it up for innocent use in the *Shepheardes Calender* ('June', l.43; see also 'January', l.58). There may also be an ironic allusion to the association of the apple with the primacy of Venus over Diana, as in Boccaccio's *Teseida* (7.61). The cherries have an iconographic connection with the church. But they are, conventionally, the 'fruit of Paradise', the soul's reward for piety and merit, as in Gorofalo's painting of the Christ-child holding a goldfinch (the soul) in one hand and offering it cherries with the other.[1] It seems straining the common meaning to identify cherries with the Roman service. Yet Spenser's way with political allegory elsewhere, the

---

[1] See Herbert Friedmann, *The Symbolic Goldfinch* (1946), p. 95. The identification of the Titaness with Arabella Stuart seems less likely as a political undertone in the *Cantos*. But see M. K. Woodworth, 'The Mutability Cantos and the Succession', *PMLA* 59 (1944), 985.

setting, and the final stanza of the episode all argue for a political interpretation roughly similar in outline to Stampfer's.

The episode has other implications: if Faunus is related to Mutabilitie in his attack on Cynthia and Order, he is related to Nature in his overlordship of the forest. Faunus is the Latin Pan, and it is possible that Spenser remembered Chaucer's use of that god in the *Book of the Duchess*, where he is referred to as 'Pan, that men clepe god of kinde' (l.521). The identification of Pan as *'totius Naturae deus'* goes back to Servius' commentary on Virgil (*Eclogues* 2.1.31), and is employed in Spenser's *Shepheardes Calender* ('May', l.54) and elsewhere. Faunus is a type of debased Nature. He presides over the forest, but his impulses serve instead of Nature's fecundity and moderation. Though Chaos has not broken his chain, as the gods feared in 6.7.14, there is something of Chaos' qualities abroad in Faunus. If the immortality of the wood-god's seed, apparently a principle of disorder, seems conducive to pessimism, it must be remembered that it is Faunus who brings about the union of Molanna with her lover. Despite Molanna's foolishness, her love for Fanchin is true, and, one may suppose from the phrase 'she herselfe doe wed', lawful. Thus Faunus, a debased Nature, serves higher purposes and Fanchin and Molanna spread themselves in 'one faire river'. This happy issue is in keeping with the traditional doctrine of Chaucer's *Parlement*, for it demonstrates impulse furthering Nature's law of love. Undoubtedly Spenser had the *Parlement* in mind and shaped his Ovidian materials to reflect the conflict between earthly and spiritual love that suffuses Chaucer's poem. These are not easily reconciled, as many episodes elsewhere in *The Faerie Queene* demonstrate. Earthly love may promote the plenitude by which imperfect, finite life gropes toward a semblance of divine infinity and completeness. But the effort must always fall short. The outcome of the Faunus episode is tragic-comic. Molanna has her Fanchin, but Faunus' salacious laughter at the central 'somewhat' of sexuality will again ring through the wood. If there is any appearance of

3

8 3 6 40

LIBRARY
College of St. Francis
JOLIET, ILL.

doctrinal indecisiveness here or in the major narrative it is resolved in the prayer with which the *Cantos* end.

c. The Narrator

The two narratives of the *Cantos* end in suspension, for the judgments of Diana and Nature permit life to continue as before. They bring about neither a tragic end nor a comic reform of the way things are. Thus the prayer, especially the last stanza, is a structural necessity and the concluding focus on the narrator wholly warranted.

The rôle of the narrator of the *Cantos* resembles that of other figures in Spenser's poetry. 'The monologue of the isolated figure, the picture of a man complaining', writes Arthos, is ever Spenser's 'controlling form'.[1] It should be emphasized that the device is a literary commonplace functioning for didactic and structural ends rather than for self-revelation.

In the *Cantos* the narrator does not passively 'frame' the two narratives; he is altered by them. In the early stanzas he gives us conventional complaints against Fortune. His initial attitude toward Mutabilitie is entirely negative, exhibited in such phrases as 'cruell sports', 'sad examples', and 'great paine'. If one were to skip to the penultimate stanza of the poem, one would discover little apparent alteration. Yet in the body of the poem the narrator does exhibit a different point of view. He shares Jove's admiration for Mutabilitie's beauty (which is not a magical or cosmetic appearance like that of Duessa or the false Florimell); he admires her boldness to the point of mocking the astonishment of the gods, and he delights in the variety she claims for herself. In the digression he depicts disobedience on earth with a hand as light as Ovid's, despite the serious political implications. Beyond this, he is moved to relate the central portion of the poem with an ebullience that suggests anything but desperation and defeat. Yet neither his complaints nor his delight are to be wholly explained by

[1] J. Arthos, *On the Poetry of Spenser and the Form of Romances* (1956), p. 22.

Nature's justification of Mutabilitie on the intellectual grounds of a slow movement of creation through temporal change to perfection. For all the many abstractions and personifications in the *Cantos*, it is the physical detail, the specific attribute, that causes the narrator's delight or dismay. If Mutabilitie's incursion and the Saviour's birth move him, they do so as palpable events, not as part of a 'trend'. In short, though he apparently accepts Nature's philosophic explanation, the narrator speaks and feels as an active, sensual man aware of his finiteness. Therefore he must remain unsatisfied with philosophic explanations and look beyond them. Hence the concluding prayer. As Whitaker observes, for Spenser 'the contemplative life of peace belongs in heaven'.[1] To reject the world in the midst of life is despair or asceticism. But the *Cantos* are climactic and eschatological. Thus the prayer is a fitting conclusion to an epic of earthly moral adventure, and serves Spenser's intention to form a Christian gentleman, who *would* presumably 'go gentle into that good night'.

The language of the prayer has evoked discussion. One cannot say with assurance whether the two spellings, 'Sabbaoth' and 'Sabaoth', are a compositor's invention or whether Spenser intended the difference in meaning between Sabbaoth ('repose') and Sabaoth ('hosts'), as in Romans 9.29. Spenser had some instruction in Hebrew at the Merchant Taylors' School and possibly knew the distinction. But despite the inconclusiveness of the evidence, one is tempted to accept Allen's reading here: that the narrator is praying not so much for a 'state of actionlessness' as 'for redemption and for admission' to the ranks of the heavenly Hosts, where he would see the panorama of the Creation as God sees it from His unmovable center.[2]

We may now return to the earlier question of the implications of the prayer. It is necessary to distinguish it from the

---

[1] V. K. Whitaker, *op. cit.*, 56.
[2] See D. C. Allen 'On the Closing Lines of *The Faerie Queene*', *MLN* 64 (1949), 93–4; L. S. Friedland, 'Spenser's Sabaoth's Rest', *MLQ* 17 (1956), 199–203.

popular view of a medieval palinode, and to note first the incorrectness of popular notions of medieval thought as a grim monolith. Ascetic rejection of the world, though often an 'official' medieval view, was hardly the only one. The biblical emphasis on God as Creator, the influence of the 'School of Chartres', and the influence of Aristotle, all promoted a more genial view of the world as an object of delight. But in any case, Spenser has not given us here a recantation like that of Chaucer's Troilus. For one thing, the world Troilus turns away from is different from the world of Faery. Though men give their hearts to faithless women in the world of Faery, it is pre-eminently the land of moral quest—of Sir Guyon and the Red-crosse Knight. It is a world both better and more important than Troilus'. In the concluding prayer we may see a turning away from the relatively good, from the process of salvation through works, in favour of the absolute goal itself. This rejection does not require a slighting of human action or passion or a simple condemnation of them. In short, the prayer is neither Puritan nor 'medieval', though it may suggest some overtones of both.

TRADITION AND CONVENTION

Read apart from the literary conventions and intellectual traditions they refresh, the *Cantos* can only be misinterpreted. *The Faerie Queene* lies on the far side of the seventeenth-century watershed of European culture, beyond Romantic notions of personal expression and sensuous realism, and beyond the neo-classic revival and alteration of formal philosophy by Descartes. Its form is governed by the artifices of decorum and rhetoric; its thought seems at times the magpie collection of what some recent commentators regret as 'a rather untidy', or 'second class', if not otiose, mind. But for Spenser, as for the early Renaissance and Middle Ages generally, truth was to be sought in 'the faithful transmission of a precious deposit', however conglomerate, and artistic excellence in 'the freedom to compete with respected prototypes', however unlike.[1] It is probably misleading therefore to speak of the 'sources' or the 'philosophy' of the *Cantos*. Both terms imply a modern particularity and personalism that Spenser would have found dismaying.

In thinking of the literary, especially the classical, antecedents of the *Cantos*, one must not imagine Spenser as typically consulting earlier authors directly. Very often, as did his contemporaries, Spenser would have depended upon the excerpts and digests of material that abounded in sixteenth-century dictionaries and commonplace collections. He undoubtedly knew Boccaccio's work on mythology and Natalis Comes' *Mythologia sive Explicationis Fabularum* (1551), and there is evidence that this treatment of the Hours in 7.7.45 took some hints from Vincenzo Catari's *Imagines Deorum* (1581), as perhaps did earlier passages in the pageant. Probably he depended also on Stephanus' *Dictionarium Historicum, Geographicum, Poeticum* (1533) in 7.7.39 and elsewhere. Though Spenser was widely read, we must think of much classical material that enters the *Cantos* as filtering through secondary works.

a. *Chaucer's* Parlement

But there is no doubt that he knew Chaucer's *Parlement of Foulys* at first-hand and well. How pervasive is Spenser's debt, Professor J. A. W. Bennett clearly indicates.

> The unfinished Mutability Cantos owe their very being to 'the Foules Parley'—which Spenser names in his poem, just as Chaucer names Alain's *Pleynt of Kynde* in his. Like the *Parlement*, the Mutability Cantos give us a debate before the great goddess, Nature; the birds—and with them all other creatures, and the gods—are arranged by Nature's sergeant, Order; even as in Chaucer each is in 'his owne place'. Spenser's

---

[1] See E. Curtius, *European Literature and the Latin Middle Ages,* trans. W. Trask (1953), pp. 597, 19. See also p. 326: 'A comprehension of the world was not regarded as a creative function, but as an assimilation, a retracing of given facts . . .'

Nature, like Chaucer's, pronounces her 'doom'; and Chaucer's simile for her surpassing beauty gives Spenser a hint for his description of her splendour; 'it the Sunne a thousand times did pass'. His Lady Nature sits upon a hill, in a pavilion not wrought by craftsman's 'idle skill', but made of dainty trees, with flowers of sweet odours at her feet; Chaucer's sits on a hill of flowers in a sweet green glade, and 'of branches were his halles and hir boures'. For her 'array' Spenser, like Chaucer, refers us to Alain. Mutability, moreover, speaks in terms that (like Theseus' peroration) are reminiscent of Cicero's doctrine as Chaucer has paraphrased it in the *Parlement* . . . whilst the two extant verses of the following canto, with their loathing of 'this state of life so tickle' . . . are in the very tone of Chaucer's African, and show the same blend of Christian and Platonic language as his concluding lines. . . .[1]

To this may be added other parallels in concept and detail. In both the *Cantos* and the *Parlement* there is the same comic exploitation of incongruities that result from giving 'human attitudes and anxieties'—in Chaucer's case to birds, in Spenser's to gods. In such details as the language of Nature's judgment, Spenser seems close to the tone of the *Parlement*. It is even possible that the unfaithfulness of Molanna was suggested by Chaucer's allusion to the story of Calyxte (l.286).

Yet Spenser is not merely the pupil. In the conception of mutability as a process of purgation and perfection, Spenser carries to fulfilment what Chaucer approached only tentatively, though it was suggested in the sources for the *Parlement*, especially in Macrobius' gloss on Cicero's *Dream of Scipio*. Moreover, the characteristic of Chaucer's way with his materials is his passion for compactness. But in Spenser, the characteristic manner is an opulent unfolding, dictated in part by the visual quality of his imagination, in part by the epic scale of his poem. And finally, the Renaissance pleasure in symbolic and emblematic presentation is, as Professor Bennett observes (p. 82), barely prefigured in the *Parlement*.

[1] J. A. W. Bennett, *The Parlement of Foules* (1957), p. 24.

b. Ovid's Metamorphoses

The Ovidian antecedent is also pervasive, and probably the particular literary model Spenser intended to outdo in his Legend of Constancie. Like his contemporaries, Spenser would have been attracted by the richly pictorial surface of Ovid's tales. In the *Metamorphoses* one finds not only the goddess Natura, but the story of the degeneration from a Golden Age and the rebellion of the giants against Jove, the Actaeon tale on which the Faunus episode is based, and the oration of Pythagoras on the mutability of the world, containing 'evidence' of the sort presented by Mutabilitie. There is even a final speech by Jove in which, after earthly mutability and disaster, Caesar and Augustus gain starry thrones and Ovid himself fame.

There are also many parallels in minor detail such as that between the story of Mutabilitie's incursions and the tale of Phaeton's ride as told by Ovid. Diana's 'shining palace', the 'silver gates', Diana's symbolic attendants, the commotion on earth, Mercury's report to Jove and the gods' assembly—all have equivalents in either *Metamorphoses* 2 or 11. In addition to Ovid's Actaeon story, there seem to be echoes of the tales of Callisto (the nymph punished by Diana in *Met.* 2.457ff.) and the rivers Alphaeus and Arethusa (*Met.* 5.572ff.). As always with such parallels, however, one must exercise caution. Some details are so much common property that they can be found in the mythological compilations, or would spring to the writer's mind without conscious intermediary.

In any case, Spenser is not Ovid. As William Nelson observes, Spenser's relation to Ovid is not one of borrower only, but of parodist. Helpless Actaeon becomes foolish Faunus; Actaeon's tragic death, Faunus' exhaustion in the woods. And Ovid's ultimate and lustful Jove becomes Spenser's middle-echelon executive with an avuncular fondness for a pretty face.

The *Metamorphoses* and the *Cantos* define one another. Ovid's mythology is a mirror that sparkles with the fact of human passion: neither with its development nor its implications, only the fact. Pythagoras' doctrine of metempsychosis in Book 15 is a coda in which, as in the tales, passion is declared immortal beyond the altering forms of flesh. For the theme of the *Metamorphoses* is not change, but persistence—Daphne's chastity in the laurel, and their lust and reluctance in the mingled form of Hermaphroditus and his nymph. This is myth emptied of its metaphysics. But for Spenser myth is a transparency through which we are to glimpse the idea of the Good. Nature's verdict reconciles the alteration of forms with the divine constancy that intends them. This is a truly archaic use of mythology, for it retains myth's earliest function as an emblem of the mysteries.

c. Other Antecedents

It would be an error to take the eighty-one items (excluding biblical references), listed in the *Variorum* 'Index of Sources and Analogues' as evidence of a merely timorous dependence in the *Cantos* on other literary works for event, tone, or phraseology.

It is safe to claim only that Chaucer, Ovid and the handbooks are important literary antecedents, and that the influence of Ariosto on narrative design and of Tasso on general moral temper is to be felt in the *Cantos* as elsewhere in *The Faerie Queene*. There are, in addition, passages that may have been influenced by Irish legends. But for all this, the *Cantos* are far more than the sum, or even only the heir, of their literary antecedents.

PHILOSOPHICAL ANTECEDENTS

Poetry, as Aristotle wrote, is closer to philosophy than to history. Yet unlike philosophers, historians and poets treat a concrete world of persons and events. The *Cantos* are didactic, but they are not a logical demonstration; they are, to use Spenser's richly connotative word, a 'fashioning'. Yet Spenser's ideas were evidently clear enough to our most 'intellectual' poet, Milton, who thought him a 'better teacher than Aquinas'. The problem of interpreting the thought of the *Cantos* is one of understanding their tradition and relating it to the age and genre in which they appear.

What it is perhaps a misnomer to call the 'philosophy' of the *Cantos* has been discussed most often in connection with specific sources. This avoids the error of presenting Spenser as an innovator. But to ally the *Cantos* too closely to the thought of a single author may have the same effect of placing him outside a tradition. His ideas are eclectic, synthetic—attempts at reconciliation. But one must also distinguish the *Cantos*, whose electicism embodies a tradition, from a pastiche like T. S. Eliot's *Waste Land*, whose allusions resound in the emptiness where a tradition no longer exists.

a. Proposed Antecedents

The intellectual 'sources' proposed for the *Cantos* have included Empedocles, Aristotle, Lucretius, Bruno, and various Renaissance Neoplatonists among others—the very number sufficient to suggest that the *Cantos* may present traditional if not perennial ideas. But to father the *Cantos* on Aristotle (because of the idea of cyclic change in *Politics* 8.12 or of the idea of a changeless bliss in *Nichomachean Ethics* 7) or on Empedocles (because of the doctrine of the four elements in *Nature* and the *Purifications*) is an arbitrary attribution of commonplaces. Greenlaw's argument that the *Cantos* are 'charged with Lucretian naturalism' is based in part on the notion that, despite Nature's verdict, 'it is clear both from the action and the trial that the true judgment is in favour of a natural law that rules gods and men alike'.[1] This simply misreads the subordinate rôle of Nature. It also neglects the implications of the Molanna story, and fails to see (as Mutabilitie herself fails to see), the religious implications of the argument from seasonal change. It is equally unlikely that the *Cantos* were conceived either in imitation of the narrative or

[1] E. Greenlaw, 'Spenser and Lucretius', *SP* 17 (1920), 455ff.

ideas of Bruno's *Spaccio della Bestia Triomphante* [R. Levinson, *PMLA* 43 (1928)], or to counter Bruno's doctrine in the *Trattato della Causa, Principio et Uno* [S. Evans, 'A Lost Poem by Edmund Spenser', *Macmillan's Magazine* 42 (1880), 150–1]. That Spenser was seriously influenced by the Neo-platonic thinkers of the Renaissance is also unlikely. He probably had a first-hand knowledge of Ficino [Sears Jayne, 'Ficino and the Platonism of the English Renaissance', *Comparative Literature* 4 (1952), 214–38], but Spenser's pre-cise knowledge of Renaissance Neoplatonism comes late in his career, and such Neoplatonic thought as his work exhibits is medieval and popular in cast rather than Renaissance and learned.[1] But this is not to deny resemblances between the *Cantos* and contemporary thought in France and Italy.

b. Some Continental Antecedents

With the poets of the Pléiade, Spenser shared a profound concern with the theme of mutability. Spenser was among the first of Du Bellay's English admirers [W. D. Elcock, *MLR* 46 (1951), 175ff.]. And Spenser's earliest published work, a group of translations for John van der Noodt's *A Theatre . . . [for] Worldlings* (1569), includes sonnets drawn from the 'Songe' Du Bellay appended to his *Antiquitez de Rome*, along with Petrarch's canzone on similar themes of earthly transience. For his volume of *Complaints* (1591), Spenser reworked his versions of the 'Songe' and the canzone, and translated the rest of *Les Antiquitez*. Some lines of the first of Du Bellay's sonnets are echoed in the *Cantos* (7.8.1–2). The 'Ruines of Rome: by Bellay' contains other tenuous suggestions of the material of the *Cantos*. Rome, 'whose high top above the starres did sore', vaguely suggests Mutabilitie; Jove fears 'least if she should greater growe / The old Giants should once againe vprise'; and the gigantomachia is presented again in stanza 12. In stanza 15 of the 'Visions of Bellay', the narrator

[1] See R. Ellrodt, *Neoplatonism in the Poetry of Spenser* (1960), especially pp. 23, 64, 211ff.

sees '*Typhaeus* sister' who 'Did seeme to match the Gods in Maiestie' and 'over all the world did raise a Trophee hie'. The narrator is 'mazed . . . with great affray' as the heavens rise against their adversary, who is struck down with thunder. Such resemblances are not offered as proof of a 'source'. They illustrate rather that Spenser's last poem is intimately related to his first, and they provide a clear example of the difference in temper between Spenser and his French antecedents. When he employs the final lines of Du Bellay's first sonnet from the 'Songe' in the *Cantos*, Spenser renders

> Puis que Dieu seul au temps fait resistance,
> N'espère rien qu'en la divinité

as

> Sith only God surmountes the force of tyme
> In God alone do stay my confidence,

Spenser changes negative to positive, hope to confidence, the vague 'divinity' to 'God', and generally exhibits, as A. W. Satterthwaite points out, the difference between his own 'militant and unwavering' Anglicanism and Du Bellay's disappointment with the Roman hierarchy. Similarly, while in a line like 'le futur est douteux, le present est certain', Ronsard, who seems to have had less influence on Spenser than did Du Bellay [Satterthwaite, *Comparative Literature* 9 (1957), 136–49], abandons an earlier hope for a perfection emerging from present corruption, Spenser holds fast to the creed, and in the *Cantos* (7.7.58) infuses it with Christian implications that contrast with Ronsard's unalloyed classicism.[1]

Comparisons of Spenser's thought and manner with that of the Italian poets of romantic epic or with Neoplatonic writers result in similar conclusions. The one to whom Spenser is closest in 'an old-fashioned simplicity of mind' is the earliest, Boiardo [H. H. Blanchard, *PMLA* 40 (1925)]. The tensions between the sensuous and the moral in Tasso are extreme and unreconciled, and they reflect anxieties over orthodoxy that

[1] A. W. Satterthwaite, *Spenser, Ronsard, and Du Bellay* (1960), pp. 31–3; 232–3.

later caused him to recast the *Gerusalemme Liberata* into (significantly) a *Gerusalemme Conquistata*, a holiness taken by force. In the *Cantos*, the effort is to reconcile rather than emasculate. One could hardly say of Spenser, as Federico Chabod says of Ariosto, that he formed with Machiavelli and Galileo part of a movement toward 'realism and individualism' that leads to the 'affirmation of the complete autonomy of art, politics, science, and history . . . to the abandonment of the typically mediaeval conception of the world according to which no branch of human activity could be considered independently of its relation to life as a whole'.[1] For Spenser, unlike his continental counterparts, the 'organically unitarian' vision one finds in the *Cantos* had not yet given way to the fragmented appraisals of experience typical of the later Renaissance. Further, Spenser had a large body of diffused Platonism at his disposal, but some resemblances between him and the Italian Neoplatonists seem fortuitous or deceptive, and the result of Spenser's heavy dependence on medieval literary traditions in which there was already a large Platonic element.

c. *Popular Medieval and Renaissance Thought*

The quasi-Aristotelian, quasi-Platonic popular tradition, on which the *Cantos* depend, merits that awkward prefix.[2] Quirks of transmission, conflation, and Christianization resulted in strange transformations of classical ideas. This was less the case with Aristotle, whose work was better transmitted, than it was with Plato, whose *Timaeus* was his only writing to exert a continuous direct influence until the translations by Ficino, completed in the 1480s. Of course, Platonism of a sort was widely available to the Middle Ages through such authors as Macrobius and Boethius, but of much medieval Platonism,

[1] F. Chabod, *Machiavelli and the Renaissance*, trans. D. Moore (1958), p. 184.
[2] A recent presentation of it is to be found in C. S. Lewis, *The Discarded Image* (1964), to which the following paragraphs are indebted. It is also dealt with briefly in another volume in this series, *The Parlement of Foulys*, ed. D. S. Brewer (1960), pp. 26ff.

Gilson has gone so far as to write that Plato himself had no part in it.[1]

Throughout the tradition there is a system of contrasts, if not of contradictions. From astronomy Aristotle derived the notion of a 'Heaven' immutable and divine; from biology the idea of a mutable, stochastic 'Nature'. In Plato's *Timaeus* there is an analogous contrast in divinity: an Idea of the Good, 'an apotheiosis of unity, self-sufficiency, and quietude', and an Idea of Goodness, of 'diversity, self-transcendence, and fecundity'.[2] These ideas are joined and elaborated greatly in popular thought. One need not search far for their relevance to the *Cantos*. On the one hand there is the world of Mutabilitie presided over by the 'highest Him', whose vicar, Dame Nature, decrees that the world continue as before; on the other there are the pillars of eternity and the Sabaoth God.

The possibility of such contrasts becoming contradictions is clear if one reflects on their implications for human attitudes. One could read out of the immutable sky and its self-sufficient God a radical contempt for the world and then opt for the contemplative life; or one could delight in the world as the beneficiary of Grace, and imitate, however modestly, the divine Creator through practical moral activity. Arguments on either side were numerous: among them that what is shifting and disunified is inferior (as in Plotinus, *Enneads* 3.7.11), an effect of the Fall; or that natural things may have merely a 'provisional or instrumental' value, leading men by contrast or by stages to the divine (as in *Timaeus* 33d); or that they may be (as Tasso wrote), the very evidence that God merits the name of Creator. The 'official' view of the medieval Church was most often on the side of contempt for the world. Yet what Lovejoy has called a 'fruitful inconsistency' was perhaps more pervasive in popular thought, and efforts were made to reconcile not only the two views, but to reconcile other-worldliness with optimism through the idea that the world, though fallen and full of evil, was a creation of the Good.

[1] E. Gilson, *La Philsophie au Moyen-Age* (1944), p. 268.
[2] A. O. Lovejoy, *The Great Chain of Being* (1936), pp. 82–83.

This fruitful inconsistency (though to call it that is perhaps begging a central question), enters of necessity into literary as distinct from more directly doctrinal works, for the imaginative writer, if only by implication, values what he expends such care in recreating. As the tradition itself has it, creation is a kind of love. So the attempt to allow room for both views, if not to reconcile them, is strong even in so Stoical a piece as Cicero's *Dream of Scipio*, in which rejection of the world is not incompatible with the injunction to win the praises of posterity by serving one's country well. Spenser would have known the *Dream*, but he would have known more intimately Chaucer's *Parlement* and Boethius' *Consolation of Philosophy*, which go further in bridging the two views of God and Nature.

To accept Chaucer's Nature, writes J. A. W. Bennett, is to reject dualism, for it is she whom Chaucer, following Alain of Lille, conceives of as 'marrying' the earthly and the divine.[1] She does this specifically through ordering all Creation, as does Spenser's Nature, in a coherent 'scale' of being, a 'great chain' in which God has demonstrated his love by exhaustive diversity (plenitude)[2] and his moral intelligence by the perfectly graded value of things from the brute material to the finely spiritual—all of them having a value proportionate to their proximity to Him.

But in Boethius, as the frequency of citation in recent criticism of the *Cantos* makes clear, the means for effecting reconciliations are more numerous and more explicit. The central problem that Philosophy must answer in the *Consolation* is the problem of the mutability of human affairs. In the course of the answer much of Spenser's materials is prefigured in Boethius' use of traditional 'topics'. Philosophy herself appears, like Spenser's Nature, both young and old; there are Fortune and her wheel, the insistence on the absence

---

[1] J. A. W. Bennett, *Parlement*, pp. 109, 124.
[2] The idea goes back to Plato's *Timaeus*, where the deity creates all things, thus exhibiting perfect love and an absence of 'envy' of any form of being. The idea is treated extensively in Lovejoy, *op. cit.*, and briefly but suggestively in relation to Shakespeare in Edward Hubler, *The Sense of Shakespeare's Sonnets* (1952), pp. 64ff.

of any crude 'poetic justice' in the world, the variety of tone from humour to exposition to exaltation. But more important than Boethius' materials are his arguments. And the most relevant of these may be stated as five propositions:

1. Fate governs the changing temporal order, but Fate itself and the order it governs are subject to Providence; thus changes are not random (IV Prose v; yet in IV Prose vi, Fate and Providence seem to be used interchangeably).

2. As a wheel's centre is motionless though its circumference moves, so Fortune, no matter what the flux of events, becomes inoperative as one approaches the divinity at its centre (IV Prose iv); hence change is not evil save as we allow it to affect us through our own distance from the deity (II Prose iv). Rather we must look on change as good, since Fortune is of God, designed for various ends, all of which are related to His patterning of things.

3. Nothing changes its essential nature (III Metre ii), and men and things inherently desire to return to their native place (the Good), which is God (II Prose ii).

4. Those who have risen to the contemplation of the Good, 'the circle of divine simplicity', must not return to worldly objects (III Prose xii).

5. We only dimly apprehend the divine vision since we exist and act in an endless flux of moments (perpetuity), whereas God exists in a limitless life outside time (eternity), which comprehends in an instant all of perpetuity (V Prose vi).

In the *Consolation* as a whole, Boethius relates the contrasting ideas of changeless Good and changing nature by presenting change as their means of union: the Good, creating nature (as in Plato) out of its goodness, moving nature (as in Aristotle) through love, and nature repaying love through a circling return to its Creator. Evil, Boethius defines, echoing Augustine in one of the master-conceptions of Christian thought, as non-being, a flight out of nature and away from that passionate mutuality between God and Creation which is the ground of being. When Mutabilitie observes of the stars and spheres that 'all that moveth, doth mutation love', she is mistaking the process by neglecting its object, for 'love seeks . . . to become as like its object as it can . . . and the nearest approach to the divine and perfect ubiquity that the spheres can attain is the swiftest and most regular possible movement, in the most perfect form, which is circular'.[1] Spenser echoes the Boethian pattern in emphasizing the cyclical return of man and nature to their divine origins.

More specifically, the propositions above suggest the grounds of the 'philosophy' of the *Cantos*. Mutabilitie is (as in 1) governed by Fate though 'the changing bond' of the temporal order itself alters. And both are governed by Providence, 'the one unchangeable direct power which gives form to all things'. Mutabilitie's 'sports' (as in 2) will seem cruel only as one allows them to seem so through failures of love and understanding. One must recognize in the transience of seasons and of men, not divine indifference or bad luck, but (as in 3) the desire of all things to return purified to their divine originals. Once having attained such insights, one must (as in 4), not fall back from them. One must be as 'Galahad, who in the attainment of his quest could finally pray that in the very joy that he then knew, in the moment of mystical illumination, he might move from earthly life to the celestial'.[2] Such is the concluding prayer, with its desire to achieve through grace a fuller vision of life from the vantage of eternity, a vision that (as in 5) one only glimpses from the midst of perpetual change.

The judgment of Nature has been singled out as the most cryptic passage in the *Cantos*. But it too yields to paraphrase on the interpretation just proposed. Change, Nature seems to say, is not the final cause or goal of temporal being. Change, as the adjective 'temporal' itself should demonstrate, is merely the mode of existence through which that being extends itself or 'dilates'. But the goal of temporal being is the return 'at length again' to its originally established form, hence to its Creator. And temporality works its 'owne perfection', its

[1] Lewis, *Discarded Image*, 114–15.
[2] Arthos, *op. cit.*, 96.

return to its divine, hence perfect, original, 'by fate', by the
equivalent of what Christians call the eternal law of God.

That Spenser knew Boethius there is no doubt. Yet it is best
to think of the two writers as mutually illuminating mirrors of
the tradition. But comparison permits us to see the *Cantos*
more clearly, not as a melancholy withdrawal, but as an ascent
to the summit of temporal experience. The pageant of change
and the prayer for its end are thus not lure and recantation,
but a single pattern—the loving return to love's source in God.

d. Contemporary Thought

Yet it is both too little and too much to find the *Cantos* merely
mirrors of the popular tradition, though it is pedantic to draw
a line between 'medieval' and early Renaissance thought,
especially in late-blooming England. There have been attempts
to locate the contemporary quality of the *Cantos* in a breakdown
of 'medieval assurance', in an 'unconvincing' affirmation of
the spiritual, especially in the concluding prayer. Such views
seem to be based on the idea that Spenser's convictions were
somehow on the side of Mutabilitie, or that they otherwise
reflected the doubts of Renaissance men 'to whom the classics
had given new values of the world'.[1] But this is reading later
intellectual developments into the poem and, in any case,
reflects an interpretation of the prayer which its tone will not
sustain.

It would be better perhaps to relate this uneasiness about
the sudden conclusion of the *Cantos* to Spenser's response to
an intellectual paradox for which Whitaker finds Renaissance
Protestantism responsible; that is, to the repudiation of the
theological basis of good works due to a hatred of indulgences,
and—at the same time—the rejection of the exclusively con-
templative as an acceptable way of life. It is obvious that the
author of the moral adventures which constitute *The Faerie
Queene* did not deny merit to works. But it is equally apparent

[1] W. C. B. Watkins, *Shakespeare and Spenser* (1950), p. 72, and
D. C. Allen, 'Degeneration of Man', 205.

4

that the Red-crosse Knight is made to doubt the value of a life
of exclusive contemplation (see *FQ* 1.10.62, 63), and this by
Contemplation himself, who addresses the Knight, signifi-
cantly, as 'thou man of earth' (1.10.52), and urges him on to
good deeds. Whether or not Anglican 'official' views were the
paradox presented above, there is no doubt that they re-
presented a shift from the 'official' medieval view, and that
the *Cantos* reflect the new emphasis: the exclusively contem-
plative life, whatever its ultimate spiritual priority, has no such
priority in the life of man on earth; and good works are now
more subject to extra-theological justifications. What these
were is clear from the political matter of the *Cantos*, and is
demonstrable from passages adjacent (1.10.55ff.) to the one
just cited. Contemplation here tells Red-crosse that he is
English, implies that Cleopolis, the city of the Faerie Queene
(Elizabeth), is a type of the heavenly Hierusalem, and identifies
Red-crosse's struggles on earth with his future in Heaven as
St George, the patron saint of the English nation. Reflecting
on their past, and influenced by Revelation and Foxe's *Book
of Martyrs*, Spenser's contemporaries came to think of them-
selves as an 'Elect Nation', destined by God to fulfil His
purpose in history.[1] For both political and theological reasons,
the Anglican Christianity to which Spenser subscribed altered
the emphasis on the active and the contemplative life from
that in the Catholicism of Chaucer's time. The Red-crosse
Knight will return to contemplation—but only after earthly
struggles. The struggle of the finite toward the good takes up
much of the poem; the prayer for contemplative existence
becomes appropriate only to the end of earthly life. These
shifts in emphasis are not a sign of a failure of 'medieval'
assurance, but of a Renaissance re-estimate of how one's faith
was to be applied. Spenser's allegory, as Kermode points out,
does not submerge events in archetypes. The Irish rebellion

---

[1] J. E. Hankins, 'Spenser and the Revelation of St John', *PMLA*
60 (1945), 364–81; W. Haller, *The Elect Nation* (1964); and especially
F. Kermode, 'Spenser and Allegorists', *Proceedings of the British
Academy* 48 (1962), 261–79.

(and the rest of contemporary politics in *The Faerie Queene*) is neither illusory nor merely illustrative.

If the poem is set apart from the medieval by its 'Protestant-imperialist' views, these views also create a different sort of tension between the real and the ideal, and between the ways of looking at each. Specifically, Spenser's outlook accepts 'the English settlement—to which as Revelation proved, all history tended, [as] a type of that final pacification at the end of time'.[1] The mutable earthly scene becomes precious, the 'Sabaoth's sight' both more precise and poignant, by reason of the continual presence of each in the other.

The language of the concluding prayer recalls the writings of Augustine. In the *Confessions* (13.36) and *Epistles* (50.9.17) he speaks, as he does in the final section of *The City of God*, 'Of the Eternal Felicity of the City of God, and of the Perpetual Sabbath'. Here Augustine asserts that the seventh age will be 'our Sabbath, which shall be brought to a close, not by an evening, but by the Lord's Day, as an eighth and eternal day, consecrated by the resurrection of Christ, and prefiguring the eternal repose, not only of the spirit, but also of the body' [trans. W. C. Greene (1960), xx, xvi–ii]. (Such references have suggested to Alastair Fowler [*Spenser and the Numbers of Time* (1964), pp. 57ff.] that the numbering of the *Cantos* is deliberate and in the tradition of medieval numerology.) But if there are resemblances between Augustine's vision and Spenser's, there are also differences. These relate precisely to the 'Protestant-imperialist' views we have just examined. Etienne Gilson tells us that under no circumstances can Augustine's earthly city, let alone his city of God, be identified with any form of the state whatever.[2] And though Augustine does of course distinguish between a good ruler and a bad, his views of secular government are far less sanguine than Spenser's. As H. A. Deane points out, the only differences Augustine finds between kingdoms

---

[1] F. Kermode, '*The Faerie Queene*, I and V', *Bulletin of the John Rylands Library* 47 (1964), 123ff.

[2] E. Gilson, *The Christian Philosophy of Saint Augustine*, trans. L. E. M. Lynch (1960), p. 182.

and robber-bands in Book IV of *the City of God* are those of size and fixed abode.[1] But for Spenser, as for many of his countrymen, Elizabeth and the English were God's special instruments for the defeat of Antichrist.

But clearer 'Renaissance' qualities in the *Cantos* are qualities of style and tone: the richer surface; the self-conscious estimate of the worth of poetry (7.1.2. and in the intent of the whole epic), and the great concern—typical of the Renaissance —with questions of the 'whatness', the process of things— though the *Cantos* still deal primarily with the question 'why'. In short, to see Spenser as dependent on a 'medieval' tradition is not to see the *Cantos* as an anachronism. But in any case, poetry, as Mallarmé said to Degas, is not made of ideas at all; it is made of words.

STRUCTURE AND STYLE

Between ideas and words there is all that the Renaissance would have called, without prejudice, the 'right artifice' of literature, its structure and style. These, too, were shaped by tradition and convention. 'Decorum' provided the writer with a sense of the tone and materials proper to each genre and theme. Traditional sources of materials, the *topoi* ('topics') or commonplaces, suggested many of the materials themselves. Conventions governing each genre, and criteria of appropriateness operating through the rules of rhetoric provided suggestions as to how materials might be presented in various *tropoi* (tropes, literally 'turns'), of phrase and thought. Beyond this there was always the prestige and challenge of classical example, from which the rules and doctrines were thought to be derived. Yet under such conditions of composition, so unlike those in force after the eighteenth century, the writer was not bound—either to succeed or to fail.

We have already noted several traditional formal elements in the *Cantos*: their organization around a debate, and the use of such familiar *topoi* as the young-old woman, and the pleasance.

[1] H. A. Deane, *The Political and Social Ideas of St Augustine* (1963), pp. 127ff.

The following remarks will hardly exhaust the stylistic conventions in the *Cantos*.

Conventions of romantic epic (though Professor Josephine Bennett has denied the existence of the form [*English Institute Essays* (1951), pp. 95–125]), are explored in works referred to elsewhere, but these affect the *Cantos* far less than they do the rest of *The Faerie Queene*. In respect to genre, however, one should be aware of the resemblances between the *Cantos* and that extensive group of medieval poems, of which Chaucer's *Parlement* is one, in which a troubled dreamer is enlightened through an allegorical vision. The *Cantos* contain something like the three sorts of dream to which, according to the classification of Macrobius, significance was to be attached. The narratives are like a *somnium*, in which truth is presented through the veil of allegory; the prayer and parts of the narrative resemble a *visio*, which presents the future; and the Judgment of Nature resembles an *oraculum*, the predictions or advice of some sage person. That Spenser presents his 'vision-poem' without the usual dream framework is due perhaps to the already dream-like ambience of the Land of Faery.

ALLEGORY AND SYMBOLISM

Macrobius' commentary on the *Dream of Scipio* provides a view of the propriety of fictions to which the *Cantos* also conforms. Only an argument grounded in truth yet exhibited through a veil of fiction is appropriate to philosophy, writes Macrobius. Moreover, the philosopher will never allow 'God, the highest and first of all things' to enter his allegory directly. It is just such a fiction that Spenser gives us. This is not the place to treat the extensive discussion of allegory that has centred on *The Faerie Queene*. Yet a brief rationale of what is sometimes scorned as 'outmoded bric-a-brac' is useful to a reading of the *Cantos*. For Elizabethans allegory was, first, a figure of speech, 'an extended metaphor'; for Spenser it was specifically 'a dark conceit'. Allegory consists in giving 'an imagined body to the immaterial' and, as C. S. Lewis points out, it is the reverse of symbolism, which views the material world as a copy of some invisible one. The distinction is useful in clarifying the special quality of the allegory in the *Cantos*.

On these definitions, the *Cantos* are both allegorical and symbolic. If they reify abstractions, the kind of natural world they present is also symbolic—a suggestion of the transcendent peace of the Sabbath's sight. The assembly of Nature, the mating of Molanna and Fanchin, even—as Millar Maclure observes—the art of the poem itself, suggest a coherence beyond the material world. In *The Faerie Queene*, the *Cantos* are almost unique in lending themselves so obviously to anagogic interpretation.

Something further should be said by way of clarifying, though not 'excusing', Spenser's use of allegory. Such excellent historical explanations as C. S. Lewis provides, or Edwin Honig's observation that through allegory Spenser revitalized a form—the romantic epic—that otherwise would have been a literary anachronism,[1] are probably not an answer to the initial doubts of the modern reader about so 'unrealistic' a literary device. The answer—if there is one apart from the excellence of the work itself—lies in an attempt to appreciate the kind of sensibility which found allegory the form most appropriate to 'philosophy'. Nowadays we distrust the idea of common experience. We decry generalizations. We are pre-occupied with the private sensibility, and admire the concreteness and particularity of the poetry which that sensibility creates. The relations between this- and other-worldliness in contemporary literature (when the writer hazards them), most often take the form of symbolism, a tentative reaching up and out that suggests a distrust of large formulations. Symbolism, then, is a 'mode of thought', but allegory is a 'mode of expression' only. It depends on one's being certain of one's views on large questions, and on accepting a subordination of the accidents of private experience to larger patterns of significance. Given such a certainty, allegory becomes the

---

[1] E. Honig, 'Recreating Authority in Allegory', *JAAC* 16 (1957), 180–93.

most direct literary method available, and it can be both precise about patterns of ideas and suggestive of a variety of illustrative patterns of experience. It is even possible to see allegory as 'a more advanced form of intellectual-artistic expression than its opposite, naturalism',[1] which is certainly closer to an unsifted, visceral response to experience. In any case, allegory denies the widespread notion of the mutual exclusiveness of poetry and knowledge, on which naturalism—the reduction of literature to sense-impressions—is based.

Though we have been properly warned to avoid reading allegory as though it were a puzzle, we cannot deny to any kind of metaphor—and allegory is one—the rôle of evoking in us a pleasurable quality of attention, a liberating disinterestedness that comes with responsible novelty, and a delight in discovering how apparent tangencies may coalesce into a resemblance. One of the delights of poetry, *the* delight for Aristotle, lies precisely in such recognition of the True behind the instanced. In the *Cantos* the combination of intellectually firm allegory with the suggestive and tentative qualities of symbolism is the appropriate vehicle for Spenser's religious stance, which permits human reason to go far, but only so far, and beyond its limits only to glimpse the ultimate.

MYTHOLOGY

Spenser's allegorical figures in the *Cantos* are largely drawn from classical mythology, and like his allegories are didactic, not decorative. 'No religion so long as it is believed, can have that kind of beauty which we find in the gods of Titian, of Botticelli, or of our own romantic poets. . . . For poetry to spread its wings fully, there must be, besides the believed religion, a marvellous that knows itself as myth.'[2] The Elizabethan use of myth was a self-conscious distancing of didactic materials. Its chief features are described in the

[1] B. H. Bronson, 'Personification Reconsidered', *ELH* 14 (1947), 163–77.
[2] C. S. Lewis, *Allegory of Love*, p. 83.

'Epistle' to Golding's translation of the *Metamorphoses*, some lines of which are an unintended gloss on Spenser's practice in the *Cantos*.

For Gods, and fate, and fortune are the termes of heathennesse,
If men usurp them in the sense that Paynims doo express.
But if we will reduce their sence too ryght of Christian law,
Too signifie three other things their termes we well may draw.
By Gods wee understand all such as God hath plaast in cheef
Estate to punish sin, and for the godly folkes releef.
By fate the order which is set and stablished in things
By Gods eternall will and word, which in due season brings
All matters to their falling out, which falling out or end
(Bicause our curious reason is too weake to comprehend
The cause and order of the same, and dooth behold it fall
Unwares too us) by name of chaunce or fortune wee it call.
                                                    (ll.320–331)

Jove and Nature are obviously among Golding's gods; Mutabilitie an aspect of his 'chaunce or fortune'. All of Spenser's mythological figures and personifications emerge from a long tradition, some of which is worth sketching in order to demonstrate the richness of connotation they would have had for an educated contemporary.

a. Nature

The universal goddess Natura was one of the last religious experiences of the late pagan world, though she had appeared often before. In Lucretius (1.21 and 2.1116), she is the creator and governor of all things, and (in 1.263), the Venus who '*aliud ex alio refecit*', dying but unaltering. In Ovid's *Metamorphoses* 15.145ff., Pythagoras describes her as '*novatrix rerum*', the renewer of the changing material forms in which the changeless soul inheres. As though subject to the goddess, her tradition alters and persists, gathering Christian meanings and descriptive concreteness.

As early as Claudian (fl.400), Nature is portrayed as ending the strife of the elements, appointing gods to serve Zeus, initiating agriculture, and wedding Proserpine to Pluto. The presence of these two, the only infernal deities allowed at

Nature's assembly, is in the tradition of Claudian, as are the functions attributed to Nature in the *Cantos*. The variety and number of creatures present at the assembly reflect Nature's embodiment of energy and love, for through her God has denied no creature existence; and also her embodiment of law, for she has ranged all her dependents 'according to their sundry kinds of features'.

For all this, Nature is not God; rather, she is 'a symbol of God's creative power' and 'of the order, stability, and beauty of the world'. Moreover, 'nothing she approves of or decides can be bad. In this representation of Nature, questions of Man's sinfulness do not enter'.[1] The formulation is as relevant to the *Cantos* as to Chaucer's *Parlement*, one of the many works in the tradition of Nature as 'the vicar of God', which culminates in Alain of Lille and continues as a Christian commonplace beyond Spenser's day. The details of Spenser's description of Nature may be tracked through these works that lead toward and away from Alain.[2]

Nature's superhuman stature is appropriately Homeric, and reminiscent, as is her ability to foretell the future, of the tutelary spirits described in Pliny and Tacitus. She is both young and old, as are Claudian's Natura and Boethius' Philosophy. Her beauty and the poet's inability to describe her recall the *Roman de la Rose* ll.16,165–9, and her veiled, mysterious quality Macrobius' commentary on the *Dream of Scipio*, 1.2.17. Her leonine face recalls Alain, and her manner of making her pavilion *The Complaint of the Black Knight*, 5.51. She gains the co-operation of Mutabilitie as Alain's Natura does that of Fortune in the *Anticlaudianus*. The comparison with the sun certainly echoes Chaucer's *Parlement*, ll.299–301, and Nature's sexual ambiguity suggests both Plutarch's description of the statue of Isis in *De Iside et Osiride*, chapter 9, and Spenser's own description of the veiled hermaphrodite Venus

---

[1] *The Parlement of Foulys*, ed. D. S. Brewer, p. 30, which also has a useful discussion of the tradition.

[2] See Curtius, *op. cit.*, chapter 6, and the valuable articles on Nature by E. C. Knowlton in *JEGP* 19 (1920); 20 (1921); 34 (1935), to which this discussion is indebted.

in *FQ* 4.10.41, another embodiment of creativity. But to identify these echoes is only to suggest the dimensions of the tradition in which Spenser worked.

More important than such details is the spirit underlying Spenser's Nature. It is the spirit of the Christian naturalism of the Middle Ages, not of the Renaissance Neoplatonism or pantheism of the Italians. We are to take seriously the biblical allusion in the last line of 7.6, and the identification of Nature's garments with the 'stuffe' Peter, James, and Mark saw on Mount Thabor (see Mark 9.2–3; Matthew 17.1–8), gracing the transfigured Christ. Nature is the vicar of a Christian God. She is able to discipline Mutabilitie, but she cannot induce in us, as may Lucretius' pagan Nature in 2.61, a serenity that puts us beyond the blows of fortune. Our knowledge of her, as it does in Boethius, must lead beyond her to the concluding prayer and to the final Author of Being.

b. Mutabilitie

Mutabilitie is the daughter of Titan, whom Jove seems to identify with Lucifer. But she is addressed also as 'daughter' by Nature in 7.59; she is immune to Mercury's snake-wreathed mace in 7.18, and her beauty is neither illusion nor deception. The inevitable quarrel over whether she is intended as a figure of good or evil has antecedents in her lineage, which is as long and complex as Nature's.

Mutabilitie is the aspect of the goddess Fortuna (probably from *vortumna*, 'she who turns the year'), as the controller of time.[1] Her history has as many vicissitudes as do her subjects. She enters myth as a goddess, and indeed, during the decadence of Rome and the early Middle Ages, she was considered an omnipotent, though degraded, form of the universal deity, more powerful even than Jove. Her appeal then was enormous. Church thinkers from Lactantius to Aquinas countered it by attacking her worship as idolatry, and

---

[1] H. R. Patch, *The Goddess Fortuna in Medieval Literature* (1927), to which the following paragraphs are indebted, traces the fortunes of Fortune through philosophy and the arts.

by declaring her an illusion, an evil spirit, and the essence of disorder. Yet she was omnipresent in the arts, and her turning wheel summarized Everyman's shrug at the unfathomable flux of history and private life. Moreover, even the Fathers needed something of the idea she embodied, for in the Aristotelian argument taken over by Augustine, chance was one of the assumptions on which free-will was postulated. It is no wonder that when the question of idolatry was largely disposed of, Fortuna was Christianized and became a servant of God. In Canto VII of the *Inferno*, Dante represents her as beyond mortal reason, reviled by men, yet unhearing, for she knows herself the agent of divine will.

This evolution of Fortune from pagan deity to Christian agency was not a smooth one, and in Machiavelli (*Prince* 25) and Bruno (*Trattato della Causa*, dialogue 5), there seems a hint of a return to the earlier pagan determinism. Machiavelli speaks of Jove himself as afraid of Fortune's power. This uneven evolution is reflected in the graphic arts. Fortune can be represented as Janus-faced, as in the twelfth-century miniature from the Codex of the Glossary of Salamon of Constance in the Munich State Library.

Spenser has taken Fortuna in her rôle as controller of Time, named her to suit his Legend of Constancie, and endowed her with qualities appropriate to his theme. Like Fortuna, Mutabilitie turns her wheel; she is also railed at by men for her cruelty and caprice; her actions are sudden and unexpected as in Chaucer's *Troilus* IV 384-5; she is haughty as in the *Roman de la Rose*, 1.6575, and wrathful; and as in *Troilus* I 848-9, if she stops her wheel she will cease to be herself. But in Spenser Mutabilitie is above all else a Christianized Fortuna, submitting her case to Nature and apparently accepting the decision. In one sense Mutabilitie is Discord, but her own arguments and Nature's verdict tell us that she is also Harmony not understood. What Panofsky says of Poussin's rendering of the symbolic figure of Time applies to Spenser's rendering of Mutabilitie: 'he does not suppress the destructive powers . . . in favour of creativeness, but merges the contrasting functions

into a unity'.[1] And, as with Poussin, the image remains a fusion
of the classical with the medieval. Both in detail and concept,
Spenser's Mutabilitie is in the medieval tradition, and the
'close connection between Love (Peace, Natura, Harmony, the
Providence of Wisdom of God) and the power of Mutabilitie,
is the medieval connection',[2] as is her connection with
Jove.

The double aspect of Mutabilitie as loyal rebel, daughter of
both Titan and Nature, enables Spenser to employ her also as
a partial image of Man. Her arguments are those of the *libertin*;
her actions those of an 'aspiring' mind. Yet she does not under-
stand what she says; the testimony she offers is against her.
And at last she is subdued by Nature's love, if not by Nature's
wisdom.

c. Jove

In the hierarchy of the *Cantos* Jove is the chief administrator
of justice under law. Such terms suggest the bureaucratic air
with which Spenser endows him. In some medieval works,
Christine's *Epître d'Othéa* for example, the planetary Jove
exhibits *pité* or *misericorde*. Some of this may be evident in
Jove's restraint in the *Cantos*. There are perhaps also sly
suggestions of the Ovidian Jove of many sexual escapades,
especially in Mutabilitie's choice of allusions and witnesses.
Jove is Nature's inferior, for she not embodies only law, but
energy and love as well. Without her aid, Jove cannot deal with
Mutabilitie, for the Titaness represents in part an innovation
of the Fall, a force that initially cracks, though it finally
confirms, the older Creation. As Spenser tells us in *FQ* 5.20.1,
'the sacred hunger of ambitious mindes' cannot be restrained
either by the laws of men or by the 'bands of nature', of which
Jove is the immediate preserver. But, the hunger is in some
sense sacred.

Throughout the *Cantos* Jove functions as planetary god for

[1] E. Panofsky, *Studies in Iconology* (1939), p. 93.
[2] Rosemond Tuve, 'A Medieval Commonplace in Spenser's
Cosmology', *SP* 30 (1933), 145–7.

the sake of the allegory, but he speaks at times like God himself.
Yet the contemporary reader was too well trained in the
complexities of allegory to mistake the poet's meaning. As
planetary God, Jove is ruler of Day and Night and father of
the Hours. Cynthia, whose function it is to carry Night's
lamp, is especially under his protection, and when she is
attacked the gods turn naturally to Jove. He is their king and
father, the dispenser of justice among them, and the chain of
necessity is tied to his seat in the heavens (*FQ* 1.5.25). Yet his
own powers are limited by Fate (*FQ* 4.2.51), so his lofty answers
to Mutabilitie must not be taken as the stance of ultimate
divinity. His rebuke may indeed read like a rebuke of the
Pelagian heresy or the Renaissance exaltation of the dignity of
man. But he misunderstands Mutabilitie almost as much as
she misunderstands herself, for she is not merely the 'off-scum
of that cursed fry'. Jove's warning that

> not the worth of any living wight
> May challenge ought in Heavens interesse

is just, but somewhat in the fashion of Polonius. And Jove's
restraint of his lightning, and his hope that Mutabilitie has
been only misled or mistaken, come from his admiration for her
person, rather than from Nature's completer understanding of
her function and Nature's completer love. With the figure of
Jove, Spenser passes beyond the use of mythic figures as
embodiments of simple forces. Jove is a dramatic, almost
'realistic', figure. His backing and filling and Mutabilitie's
misdirected arguments are essentially comic devices. They
place us above the clash of cosmic powers, and enable us to
look down on it with something of Nature's cheerfulness.

d. Other Uses of Mythology

Spenser employed mythology for effects that would have been
otherwise difficult to achieve. To have said that Arlo-hill was
'godforsaken' after Molanna's betrayal would have been
doctrinally incorrect. But the mythological apparatus of the
poem permits Spenser to achieve with doctrinal safety

something of the effect of that adjective through Diana's departure from the woods. A more striking use of myth is to be found in the sudden crystallization of the poem's meaning in the allusion to the wedding of Peleus and Thetis, that goddess of many changes, when Apollo himself 'did sing the spousall hymne full cleere'. In the *Ovide Moralisé en Prose*, the marriage of Peleus and Thetis is allegorized as the prelapsarian union of man and god. However, the theme antedates medieval reinterpretations of myth, and in its classical forms is even more relevant to the theme of the *Cantos*. In Catullus the Fates themselves sing at the feast, and the poet speaks of the 'lot of happy Peleus . . . before contempt of piety began'. The precise nature of this Golden Age, however, is suggested by a line in Ovid which may well have rung in Spenser's memory during the composition of the twelfth stanza. When the human Peleus sought instruction as to how to subdue the changing goddess, he was told that, though Thetis were to take a hundred false forms, he was to hold her tightly until she took again the form she had at first (*Met.* 1.253-4). The allusion thus may look forward to the judgment of Nature as well as back to the Golden Age. And the marriage of Peleus and Thetis—of man to god at the end of alteration— is the union desired in the concluding prayer. As throughout the *Cantos*, Spenser has here employed myth with ingenuity and care to contain, rather than merely decorate, the theme of the poem. The richness of the allusion to Peleus' story is increased if one recalls that only a few lines later in Ovid his happiness, ended by his crime, is restored through the inter- vention of the goddess to whom he has been joined.

The special character of Spenser's myth-making in the *Cantos*, as in *The Faerie Queene* in general, deserves comment. In English literature it is very nearly unprecedented. In most narrative, varieties of human experience are related so as to suggest—as in Joyce—the pattern of a myth. But Spenser relates his myths so as to suggest the varieties of human experience. The effect is one of enriching the significance of fable rather than of contracting the significance of events.

Later attempts to achieve it as in, for example, Tennyson's 'Demeter and Persephone', show the extent of Spenser's art.

ICONOGRAPHY, IMAGERY, AND EMBLEMS

It will perhaps seem odd to consider the imagery and iconography of the *Cantos* under the rubric of tradition and convention. Whether taken loosely as verbal picture or narrowly as metaphor, imagery is expected nowadays to convey immediate, if not private, sensuous experience. This view would have been strange to Spenser. Renaissance imagery was expected to satisfy the criteria of significance and decorum. And in an age when information was less extensive and more directly connected to cosmological or religious ideas than in our own, both criteria promoted the formation of clusters of conventional imagery, which not only evoked but taught. The iconography of the seasonal pageant—whose details are indispensable to an understanding of the *Cantos*—exemplifies this.

Spenser's pageant of the Months and Seasons reflects an iconographic tradition rooted in the classical view that different portions of time had different qualities assigned by Zeus, and reinforced in medieval poetry. Knowing that nature was created by God, the medieval poet could therefore address its component parts as creatures of God or Christ. It is unnecessary to stalk Spenser's pageant to particular sources. The personification of seasons and months was inescapably part of the conventions of religious art. 'Didactic exposition . . . of the mutation of the year' was the characteristic development of 'English seasons-description from before Lydgate until after Spenser', and the basic concept of such description, the unity of God and Creation, was 'often given a Neoplatonic exposition'.[1] Spenser's readers would have understood, then, that Mutabilitie's witnesses, though called for the plaintiff, could testify for the defense.

The pageant of the Seasons demonstrates, not randomness,

[1] Rosemond Tuve, *Seasons and Months* (1933), pp. 122, 126. The accretion of iconographic detail is traced pp. 122ff.

but order—in plant, in man (there is a suggestion in the Seasons of the Four Ages of Man theme), even perhaps in the history of cultures, for conquest and labour are followed by plenty and dissolution. The progression of the Months is even more eloquent testimony that Mutabilitie is the instrument of higher law. March, not January, enters first. Spenser employed the legal, rather than the popular, calendar year, because it begins with the month of the Annunciation (Lady Day is the 25th), which also began the Christian era and, according to patristic authority and classical belief, was the first month of the Creation and of history (see *Exodus* 12.2). Spenser's use of the 'Year of Incarnation' or 'Year of Grace' as it was called, enabled him to harmonize nature and grace as he had already done in the figure of Nature. Further, the descriptions of the Months embody in detail the pattern of God's redemptive plans, 'for the circle [of months], like the zodiac, is the emblem of perfection; it is also the symbol of eternity. In the circle of Spenser's calendar, with its counterpoint of labours and virtues, we see the eternal purpose Incarnate in time'.[1]

In the pageant of the Months, human labour is directed toward harvest, but, allegorically, labour, Adam's punishment, is directed toward a harvest of the spirit: the return of Astraea, virgin goddess of innocence and purity, who had fled the earth after 'Wrong was lov'd and Iustice solde'. That beyond even this harvest, and beyond the birth of Christ, lie January and February, bitterly cold and near death, but bearing hatchet and plough, suggests the need for further labour to prepare for a 'hasting Prime' beyond the cycle of earthly months—a renewal whose harvest is the theme of canto VIII.

Redemption through labour is not the only aspect of the divine plan which the pageant sets forth in conventional iconography. There is also a pattern of human love and divine justice. These are arranged in a sequence which suggests the obvious Christian values. From the seed merely broadcast and

[1] Sherman Hawkins, 'Mutabilitie and the Cycle of the Months', in *Form and Convention in the Poetry of Edmund Spenser* (1961), ed. W. Nelson, pp. 91, 96. This essay contains an examination of the pageant to which the following paragraphs are indebted.

the womb of earth viewed only in terms of 'fruitfull hope of nourishment' (March) a thematic thread runs to the wanton Kid and the rape of Europa (April). Then to the 'fayrest mayd' (now the month, May, itself), fluttered round by Cupid and supported by the Gemini, whose presence recalls the rape of Leda, and identifies the 'fayrest maid' as Helen, who was the daughter of Leda and Sister of the Twins. The reference to the maid's being treated 'like to their soueraine Queene' is a reminder of Cynthia-Elizabeth in canto VI, since the laughter that greets the maid is precisely the salacious hilarity of Faunus. In June and July the thread seems broken, though the hypocrisy and nudity they represent are equally aspects of imperfect earthly love. In August, however, the theme returns with the return of Astraea, the 'lovely Mayd' and 'righteous Virgin'. There is further elaboration of the compliment to Elizabeth here. She had been represented as Astraea before, and Spenser had alluded to the Queen in the person of Belphoebe (see *FQ* 2) to illustrate virginity as a necessary mode of love.[1] So in the pageant Elizabeth appears as the referent of the two Venuses: the celestial Venus (August) and the Earthly Venus (May).

With the coming of Astraea, the pageant (despite October's almost obligatory alcoholic lust), no longer emphasizes the sexual aspect of human love, but the aspects that unite it to divine love, Justice. These are embodied in Astraea herself, in September's 'paire of waights', in October's mastery of the 'dreadfull Scorpion', who was the instrument of Diana's injustice, and in the birth of the Saviour. The awkward possibilities of December's Goat (the goat was a 'type' of lechery), are avoided by making him the instrument of the charity (another aspect of higher love) shown to the infant Jove, who was nursed on goat's milk by the nymph Amalthea. The story was traditionally associated with this sign of the Zodiac, and relates to myths about the preservation of the infant sun-god during the winter solstice. Here it has overtones

[1] See F. A. Yates, 'Queen Elizabeth as Astraea', *Journal of the Warburg and Courtauld Institutes* 10 (1947), 27–82.

appropriate to the Christ-child's birth in a manger. The
theme culminates in the divine love implied in the hasting
Prime, the renewal for which February prepares after the
purging away suggested in January's 'Romane floud'.

Thus the pageant suggests a hierarchy of love embodied in
seasonal mutation. It suggests also the ages and duties of
individual men, and in a general way, the history of Man from
Creation through the coming of Christ to the 'Prime' that lies
beyond temporality. All these were conventional meanings of
the iconography of the months.

Other iconographic details also weaken Mutabilitie's case
by demonstrating order and control in the universe. Those
animals traditionally associated with evil or evil passions in
myth, legend, or animal lore are tamed by their riders. Thus
April rides Europa's Bull (lust), June the Crab (deceit),[1] July
the Lion (wrath), October the Scorpion (thought by astrologers
to be the source of war and discord), and November the
Centaur. Despite the legendary wisdom of Chiron, Centaurs
were generally employed in Christian iconography as symbols
of Evil (as in Oreagna's depiction of Hell in the Or San Michele
in Florence), or of savage and unnatural lust (see *Lear* 4.6.126).
Moreover, astrologers were convinced that men strongly
influenced by Scorpio and the Centaur were likely to be
deceitful. In the pageant, these animal Vices do not dominate
their zodiacal regions, but are dominated by men.

The pageant closes on a summary of such meanings. The
Hours were the doorkeepers of Heaven, charged with super-
intending the elevation of heavenly bodies over the horizon
and, by extension, with bringing out the circle, or completion,
of events.[2] It is appropriate that they are followed by Life and
Death, which summarize the fate of man as it is presented in
the pageant of the Seasons and Months. For Death, though
grim, is 'but a parting of the breath',—and Life has 'wings of

---

[1] The crab was also associated with inconstancy; see Peacham's
Minerva Britanna (1612), p. 147.

[2] See A. Kent Hieatt, *Short Time's Endless Monument* (1960),
chapter 3, and Appendix for Spenser's conception of the Hours.

gold fit to employ'. Though fleeting, it is a precious instrument.

Most of the iconographic details of the pageant were readily available to Spenser in the traditions of the zodiac, in the representation in art and pageant of the months and seasons (especially in Ovid), and in the emblem tradition. There is also a lineage for the particular use to which Spenser put the pageant. Virgil contributed allegory to pastoral and so modified the eclogue to admit its use as a context for conflicting ideas. From the allegorized eclogue, the medieval *débat* emerges by way of the *conflictus*. And from débats such as Chaucer's *Parlement of Foulys* come the *Cantos of Mutabilitie*.[1]

For all this, Spenser's use of the iconographic tradition is more than adroit aping. Tradition confers no immunity against artistic failure. Particularly impressive is the comic invention: the pageant is Mutabilitie's case and, even more, its own rebuttal. Second, the traditional materials are renewed by the poet's exquisite choice of language and figure. There are also what seem to be iconographic innovations, as in June, represented as a Player, whose motion on the Crab is compared to 'Bargemen . . . like that ungracious crew which feigns demurest grace'. In any case, the whole is more than the sum of its traditions, abounding in verbal and human energy, yet functioning economically in the narrative.

Another reflection of the close link between theme and figure in the *Cantos* is found in their dominant image, the circle. 'If we stand back from Spenser's *Mutabilitie Cantos*', writes Northrop Frye, 'we see a background of ordered circular light and a sinister black mass thrusting up into the lower foreground'.[2] Less fanciful, perhaps, are the presence of the ever-whirling wheel of the first line, the circle of the Moon, and other uses of the image, implied at least, in the wheel of Ixion and the great cycles of man and nature. It is appropriate that the circle, the figure of motion in resolution, should dominate

---

[1] Tuve, *Seasons and Months*, pp. 34–5; J. H. Hanford, 'Classical Eclogue and Mediaeval Debat', *Romanic Review* 2 (1911), 16–31, 129–43.

[2] Northrop Frye, *The Anatomy of Criticism* (1957), p. 140.

a Legend of Constancie (whose own emblem was the circle-making compass),[1] for the burden of such a legend would be divine stability in the flux of existence. The circle was an inevitable choice; religion itself is a 'binding back', and the use of circular figures in mystery and ritual dates from antiquity, as do the wheel of fate, the circle as the form of the heavens, and as the symbol of eternity. Other images in the *Cantos* also convey the poet's theme. As we have seen in the examination of iconography, 'Every image and epithet . . . is heightened by the constant presence in our minds of the nature of the philosophical problem presented'.[2]

The imagery of the *Cantos* satisfies equally the criterion of decorum. In most instances this is obvious. But in a line like,

Bade her attonce from heauens coast to pack

the picture evoked seems to diminish the ethereal region to a merely mortal shore and Mutabilitie's attack to boarding-house scandal, apparently inappropriate to the theme of the *Cantos* or to the person of the Moon goddess. Yet Miss Tuve finds the ironic and superficially indecorous images in the *Cantos* to be examples of a widespread strategy found also in the debate-poems of Marvell and Daniel. 'Despite the necessities imposed by the epic form (on tempo and pace especially), the rough insolence of some of the images and the insinuating quality of others reveal the normal effect of meiosis, in this earliest important attempt to state seriously in poetry the accusations later so common in *libertin* thought.' The intention governing the use of the 'figure of diminishing' is ironic. One meiosis counters another, 'and in each case the nature of this figure operates as a criticism of the opposing position'. Thus Cynthia's speech conveys her understanding of how completely Mutabilitie's rebellion is the reverse of the heroic effort she imagines it.

Another and related consideration operates in Spenser's ironic figures. The gods of the *Cantos* are not God. When

[1] See Rosemary Freeman, *English Emblem Books* (1948), p. 23 for the figure.
[2] Tuve, *Elizabethan and Metaphysical Imagery*, p. 160.

Spenser compares them to a 'sort of Steeres', standing cow-eyed and open-mouthed at Mutabilitie's daring, he is concerned to indicate the precise plane on which the action of the *Cantos* takes place. The figure evokes, though the Homeric epithet 'ox-eyed' (or 'ox-faced') Hera, a lively sense of the difference between the Christian God and these classical surrogates. The clash between Mutabilitie and these godlings is in the nature of a joke to the very Highest. The poet's faith is strong enough to free him for the ironies that play about even the highest agents.

In form Spenser's imagery is emblematic 'in the sense that the image and its significance are clearly distinguished from each other, and the likenesses are established point by point between them'. These may be implicit rather than explicit, but there is no attempt at identification or fusion of the image with its object. The appropriateness of emblem to allegory is, on this definition, obvious, as is the appropriateness of the emblem to Spenser's specific way of working with allegory which, as we have noted earlier, does not dissipate individual experience in an archetype. The use of emblems, Rosemary Freeman remarks, leads to a preference for simile over metaphor, and to the consequent use of largely visual imagery.[1] The critical objections this has led to will be examined later in the discussion of rhetoric. But for the present it is enough to assert the decorum and significance of Spenser's imagery, and its subordination to his theme and genre. In the comparison between Diana and the dairy-maid, he even employs an 'epic simile', though, appropriately, a comic one.

THE STANZA

As is the rest of *The Faerie Queene*, the *Cantos* are cast in a nine-line stanza, interlacing three rhymes and resolving eight pentameters in a twelve-syllabled alexandrine. The stanza is rightly called Spenserian, for its aural opulence, its length, and its unification of diversity are qualities characteristic of Spenser's art. Yet the stanza-pattern resembles *rime royal*,

[1] Freeman, *op. cit.*, 103.

ottava rima, Chaucer's 'Monk's Tale' stanza, and both the rhyme-scheme and organization of the Italian sonnet. Disputes over its origins, however, or over the relative influence on Spenser of French, Italian, and native precedent are not to be resolved, nor are they crucial.

More to the point is the question of the appropriateness of the stanza to narrative poetry. Jonson disliked it, and the disputants in Harington's *Metamorphosis of Ajax* (1596) complained that the 'last verse disordered their mouths'. Pope, in a famous parody, asserted that

> A needless alexandrine ends the song
> That, like a wounded snake, drags its slow length along,

and Thomas Warton that the stanza invited circumlocution, redundance and puerility. More recently Derek Traversi has detected in the stanza a languidness and enervation at odds with Spenser's moral purpose.[1] Defences of the form are equally vehement. It is especially significant that such different poets as James Beattie, who employed the stanza in *The Minstrel* (1771–4), and Shelley, who used it notably in *The Revolt of Islam* and *Adonais*, should have chosen precisely the same phrase—'magnificence of sound'—in justifying it. Perhaps most telling, on both sides of the question, is Shelley's remark that the Spenserian stanza is a 'better shelter for mediocrity' than either Shakespearian or Miltonic blank verse. Objections to the stanza seem at bottom objections to the long poem. That 'Homer nods' is not a weakness, but a condition, of epic, in which the sustained intensity of lyric would be intolerable, were it possible. Hence the usefulness of Spenser's invention: its couplet termination allowed vignettes, setting off phases of action, description, or thought; its alexandrine mitigated the tendency of the English pentameter couplet to decisive closure, thus permitting the poet—as Saintsbury observed—to launch one stanza forward into the next; its richly echoing rhymes

[1] Comment on the stanza is conveniently gathered in B.E.C. Davis, *Edmund Spenser* (1933), 202ff. Traversi's remarks appear in *The Age of Chaucer* (1954), ed. Boris Ford, pp. 213–38.

redeemed passages which the need for exposition or for a bland, contrasting texture might have condemned to drabness.

Spenser countered one disadvantage of the stanza for narrative—the danger of its falling into lyric isolation—not only through the logic and forward motion of tale and argument, but through syntactical and rhetorical links (7.6.48–9, 7.7.14–15), rhyme-echoes, assonance, or alliteration (7.6.35–6, 7.6.45–6, 7.6.50–1, 7.7.5–6–7), and the more obvious devices of relative pronoun, binding conjunction (7.7.10–11), and relating word (7.7.33–4).

But the chief danger in the stanza—the temptation it offers both poet and reader to linger over the sound, rather than the gist, of language—was intensified by Spenser's management of the iambic line.

METRE AND SOUND

In the *Mutabilitie Cantos* one finds enjambement (7.6.1.1, 4), though relatively infrequently; the substitution of an accented for an unaccented syllable at the opening of the line (7.6.3, 2, 8); appropriate clusters of heavily (7.6.22.2) or lightly accented (7.6.52.2) syllables; lines with feminine endings (7.6.8.2, 4, 7); or with additional unaccented syllables (7.6.10, 8), and great variation in the management of internal pauses, especially in the alexandrine. But as metrical performance, the *Cantos* stand at a pole opposite to the 'irregularity' of Donne's *Songs and Sonnets*. The actual cadences of Donne's lines reach toward the vivacity of speech, those of Spenser toward the ceremony of the iambic norm. This is wholly appropriate both to Spenser's serious aim, to the romantic ambience of his epic, and to the epic genre itself. Donne's dramatic and 'realistic' handling of metre would have led logically, in a long narrative, to prose.

It follows that the reader will encounter little difficulty with Spenser's metre, whose regularity arises from, though it also occasionally distorts, the conventional stress of words. In sounding 'ancient' (7.6.2.2) as trisyllabic, or 'deemed' (7.6.11.9)

as bisyllabic, or 'tortious' (7.6.10.6) as either, for no reason
other than that of smoothness in the reading, one will be
adopting the attitude of Spenser himself who (unlike his
friend Harvey or Gascoigne, both of whom urged a 'normal'
accenting, even for classical verse) saw no reason why 'rough
words' could not be 'subdued with use'. Lines are frequently
regularized in the *Cantos* by -*ed* endings which have the force
of syllables and a slightly archaic effect.[1] Smoothness dictates
the synaloepha in 'th' Aire' (7.7.25.6), and the failure to elide
'to Aire' in the same line, as it does the aphaeresis of ' 'mongst'
in 7.6.2.4. Archaic spellings do not trouble the metre; on the
contrary, the archaic prefix *y*- in present participles, and the
then obsolescent suffix -*en* on infinitives and other forms
(7.7.53.4), and coinages in an archaic spirit (such as 'addoom'
in 7.7.56.8), have an obvious metrical utility. The rule of
thumb in reading the *Cantos* aloud is that tact should always
be exercised to draw the speech stress toward the iambic norm.
In this there is little difficulty, since Spenser's metre is rarely
Procrustean, and his use of archaism, coinage, and variant
forms shapes the language to the metre. The alexandrine,
however, can be more than a mouthful in English. It is sounded
most easily when the pause comes, as it does typically, after
the sixth syllable. But even when the pause is appropriately
repressed (7.6.9.9) or doubled for rhetorical effect (7.6.37.9),
or placed to isolate a phrase, the line is readily harmonious, its
parts usually contrasting in rapidity or weight (as in 7.6.52.9),
for a discernible effect.

Yet Spenser's relative avoidance of metrical variety does not
often result in dullness. The alexandrine continually refreshes
the pentameters. Further, the rhythmic unit of the *Cantos* is
not the line, but groups of lines or even whole stanzas, whose
qualities are set off against one another (as in 7.6.30–1). And,
as Catherine Ing points out,[2] 'the verse's freedom from

---

[1] The frequency of the sounded -*ed* is overwhelmingly greater in
Spenser than in Shakespeare, Kyd, or Marlowe. See H. Sugden, *The
Grammar of The Faerie Queene* (1936), p. 102.
[2] Catherine Ing, *Elizabethan Lyrics* (1951), p. 219.

unprepared for rhythmic changes' is a freedom to render fully the pitch and character of sounds from whose relations the singing quality (which Dryden and others thought to rival Virgil), derives.

The aural texture of the *Cantos* runs the gamut from the consonantal Billingsgate of 'this off-scum of that cursed fry' (7.6.30.1), to the lyric vowel sequence of 'Out of her bowre, that many flowers strowes' (7.6.41.5). Alliteration and internal rhyme or assonance, despite the strictures of some contemporaries against them, are favourite Spenserian devices. Hardly a line in the *Cantos* is without one or another. They not only organize stanzas, but they link them. Rhetorical figures that required repetition of sounds or rhythms are also frequent in the *Cantos*. Among them are the polyptoton (Puttenham's 'translacer') of 7.7.14.1–2, the chiasmus of 7.7.58.8–9, the asyndeton of 7.7.50.8, the polysyndeton of 7.7.25.6–9, the pleonasmus of 7.6.2.29, and the anadiplosis of 7.7.46.1–2, to cite only a few. As early as 1589 Puttenham was condemning the overuse of such figures of repetition, and Spenser's dependence on them is one of the conservative aspects of his style. Yet the vogue long had its defenders, among them Peacham, who emphasized the logical utility of repetition with variation.[1]

W. B. C. Watkins' observation that sound relations in Shakespeare are characteristically puns, while those in Spenser are characteristically internal rhymes (7.6.51.3: shame-game) or echoes (7.6.47.5, 6: sight-sought, larke-looke) suggests the strength and weakness of Spenser's manner.[2] The manner, however, is fully intended, and the aural opulence permitted by the interlaced rhymes and the regular, almost 'square',

---

[1] On this point see Sister Miriam Joseph, *Shakespeare's Use of the Arts of Language* (1947), p. 307. This work contains convenient definitions of the rhetorical terms used in this and later sections.

[2] W. C. B. Watkins, *Shakespeare and Spenser* (1950), p. 286. This view is somewhat modified by Linwood Orange's careful studies in 'Spenser's Word-Play', *N&Q*, n.s. 5 (1958), 387–9 and in his Duke University dissertation (1955) on the same subject. Yet Watkins' point is generally correct.

handling of metre can result in rude vigour as well as delicacy. Yet the reader might well remember the inferences to be drawn from the remarks of Jonson [*Works* (1947), 7.618], whose verse technique falls midway between that of Donne and Spenser. Edwin Morgan, writing as if in Jonson's person, has judiciously teased out these inferences:

> I know very well how attractive in this poet is the habit of *appearing* to communicate a great deal by the rhapsodical sweetnesses of the rhythms of stanzas and of individual concatenations of sounds, but it is surely an uncritical appreciation to *assume* the sense from an *assumed* knowledge of the sensuous manner in which verse works, and I would therefore have you read him rather as you would prose, with the mind strained for meaning, rather than the ear for an ambiguous deliciousness.[1]

Spenser's option for ceremonious musicality against realistic or dramatic spareness involved not only a rejection of Gascoigne's view that polysyllables were un-English and cloying, but a partial rejection of his own previous experimentation in the *Shepheardes Calender*. Yet the style of *The Faerie Queene* does not isolate him (as is sometimes asserted), from the main literary developments of his age. His peculiarly musical verse and his emblematic presentation of the action of *The Faerie Queene* are in accord with current standards of decorum and significancy. And they document the shift from an aural to a visual culture taking place during the early Renaissance. Both exhibit also Spenser's rôle as the innovator who preserves.

In some respects, however, the *Cantos* are freer in metre than the rest of *The Faerie Queene*. Professor Padelford (*Variorum* 6.445ff.) found relatively more run-on lines and a greater variation of tempo and flexibility of tone than in the earlier books. The *Cantos* 'are sown with the interruptions of *utterance*': explanatory phrases (7.6.8.5–7), opposition (7.6.22.2–4), apostrophe (7.6.49.6), rhetorical question (7.6.36.6) and aside or *sotto voce* (7.6.26.7–8). All these testify,

---

[1] Edwin Morgan, ' "Strong Lines" and Strong Minds', *Cambridge Journal* 4 (1951), 481.

if not to rapidity of composition, at least to the dramatic confrontation the *Cantos* present.

DICTION

Spenser's tireless ease with his difficult stanza was furthered by the liberties he took with diction, liberties sufficient to provoke Jonson's famous observation that Spenser 'writ no language'. One such liberty, not infrequently employed in his day, was classified under the varieties of metaplasm—our 'poetic license'—whereby language was adapted to metre and rhyme through the 'transformation of Letters, or sillables . . . contrary to the common fashion of writing or speaking'.[1]

a. Metaplasm

The common varieties of metaplasm are present in the *Cantos*. Syllables or letters are added (prosthesis) or subtracted (aphaeresis) at the beginnings of words, as in 'yborne' and ' 'mongst'.[2] They are added (epenthesis) or subtracted (syncope) in the middle of words, as in 'lightened' (7.6.9.8) and 'count'nance', and added (paragoge) or subtracted (apocope) at the end of words, as in 'dew-full' and 'Dayr' (7.6.48.4) and 'whist' (7.7.59.6). In addition, the *Cantos* provide examples of elision when two vowels come together (synaloepha), as in 't'envie', and of the substitution of letters (antisthecon), as in 'teld' (7.6.27.9) and 'rade' (7.7.41.5). There is a transfer of letters (metathesis) as in 'brast' for 'burst', here coupled with antisthecon. The substitution of long for short or stressed for unstressed syllables (diastole), and its opposite (systole), are exemplified by 'wend' for 'weened' and by 'Empíre' (7.6.21.4). In 7.6.33.7, however, 'Empire' is apparently to be accented as

---

[1] Henry Peacham, *The Garden of Eloquence* (1577), sig. E v.

[2] Line references are provided where the example would be difficult to understand out of context. Some instances of metaplasm are less daring than they may first appear. For example, the syncope 'physnomy' is not a contraction from the modern 'physiognomy', but from variants like 'phizonomye', which the *OED* ascribes to Caxton in 1489.

it is today. Again, Spenser's practice is less of a distortion than it may appear to be at first; one must recall the relatively greater strength of secondary stress which persisted into the seventeenth century.

In addition to metaplasm Spenser employs varieties of enallage (the substitution of one case, tense, person, gender, number, or mood for another), as in the plural 'wealths' (unless this is a compositor's error, as some editors have supposed), and in 'dare' as the verb whose subject is 'off-scum' (7.6.30.2), and in the phrase 'the highest him'. He also employs anthimeria (the exchange of parts of speech), as in 'foul' (7.6.49.3) and 'short' (7.6.51.7) as adverbs.

Yet such examples should not leave the impression that Spenser's diction is gnarled or eccentric. Nor are they peculiar to Spenser. Sidney, for instance, may be considered something of an innovator in rhyming almost always with complete phonetic accuracy and hardly ever allowing himself the common licence of antisthecon. In any case, Spenser's metaplasm does not lead to unclarity. A remark of the late Percy Long [*MLR* 12 (1917), 88]—that in modernized spelling a page of *The Faerie Queene* might seem less remote than a page of Shakespeare—applies as well to Spenser's metaplasm as to his archaism. Beyond this, one ought to recall the large number of acceptable variants in both spelling and pronunciation common in Standard (London) English in Spenser's day. The most extensive study of Spenser's orthography concludes that even in the *Calender* Spenser rarely departed from what would have been acceptable diction in the milieu in which he had been raised.[1] But one must remember that one is not always dealing directly and exclusively with Spenser's own spelling when one reads the *Cantos* or, indeed, any part of *The Faerie Queene*. The analysis of documents in Spenser's hand ('hands' would be better since he wrote English in both an Italian and a 'secretary hand', as well as employing a quite different hand for Latin), shows Spenser to have been both 'modern' and

[1] Gladys D. Haase, 'Spenser's Orthography', unpublished Columbia University thesis (1952), 60–1.

systematic in his spelling. In fact, he was evidently more 'modern' and more consistent than were those who set his poems up in type.[1] This should be taken into account in the following discussions on archaism in diction and applied to the previous discussion of the aural qualities of the verse.

b. Archaism,[2] Dialect, and Coinage

To conservative nationalists who disapproved of 'oversea' language, and to those who wished to purify or standardize the mother tongue, revival and innovation in diction would have seemed corruptions. To humanists vain of their avant-garde classicism, as was Gabriel Harvey, Spenser's archaisms would have been further evidence that he had permitted 'Hobgoblin to runne away with the garland from Apollo'. But such classicist views were more 'classical' than those of the Greeks, for Aristotle himself (*Poetics* 1485a,b) recommended metaplasm, coinage and other departures from current diction as proper to the lofty style of epic. Unlike the poets of the Pléiade, who also approved of archaism, Spenser employs it, not primarily to enlarge the resources of the language, but to serve the decorum of particular poems. Where archaism is inappropriate, as in the *Fowre Hymnes*, he avoids it.

The archaism of the *Cantos* is an aid to metre, as in the archaic *y-*, and to rhyme, as in words like 'stoures'. More important, such archaisms extend the decorum of the poem into its diction. They create a proper ambience, remote and suggestive, for Spenser's ladies, gentlemen, and beasts. And the idealism of the poem merges naturally with the nostalgia which the archaism fosters.

If we cannot go quite as far as Percy Long in thinking Spenser's archaism largely an appearance, a matter of spelling

[1] R. M. Smith, 'Spenser's Scholarly Script and "Right Writing" ', *Studies in Honor of T. W. Baldwin*, ed. D. C. Allen (1958), p. 97 and *passim*.
[2] The subject is treated in B. R. McElderry, 'Archaism and Innovation in Spenser's Poetic Diction', *PMLA* 47 (1932); E. F. Pope, 'Renaissance Criticism and the Diction of The Faerie Queene', *PMLA* 41 (1926), and V. Rubel, *op. cit.*

only, we can observe that, apart from unique rhymes, Spenser's verbs are as regular as Shakespeare's, that the total number of archaisms is quite small, and that, in short, his vocabulary is that of his contemporaries.[1] The archaism of the *Cantos* affects vocabulary, spelling, inflection, and syntax in order of decreasing importance. Inevitably Spenser's diction must seem more archaic to our century than to his, and it is not always possible to distinguish among deliberate archaisms, obsolescent words whose frequency in Spenser imparted in the early 1600s only the suggestion of a patina, and words which only subsequently acquired their archaic flavour. Though 'eke' as 'also' is used four times in the *Cantos* and only three in all Shakespeare, it was current in 1580. 'Sith', referring to time, was a deliberate archaism. Yet in Shakespeare one finds twenty examples of it in reference to cause. 'Eft' and 'eftsoons' (two and four appearances respectively in the *Cantos*, and the latter only once in Shakespeare), were not archaic, yet their frequency in Spenser must have seemed old-fashioned at least. Though E. K.'s glossing of 'eld', 'hent', 'mell', 'reck', 'sheene', and 'uncouth' for the *Shepheardes Calender* was probably pedantic, these words, which appear in the *Cantos*, were possibly also becoming old-fashioned.

Among the deliberate archaisms of the *Cantos* are 'behight', 'bowre', 'breem', 'doom' (as 'judgment'), 'emprise' (a favourite of Chaucer), 'hight', 'inly', 'nathlesse', 'nathemore', 'whilere', 'whilom', 'yfere' (which would have been recognized as a common rhyming-tag of medieval verse), and 'yode' (an instance of archaic inflection). To this list one might add further examples of archaic inflection in both nouns and verbs, though these are often difficult to distinguish from metaplasm. In all there are probably fewer than eighteen words in the *Cantos*—apart from inflected forms—that can be called deliberate archaisms. And both these and Spenser's use of old inflections demonstrate his quite accurate knowledge of

[1] Sugden, *op. cit.*, 10, puts the number of archaic nouns and verbs in the whole *Faerie Queene* as 'not over one hundred'; McElderry, *loc. cit.*, 168, places the total for all archaisms at about 320.

medieval authors, rather than the ignorance attributed to him by nineteenth-century philologists.[1]

Spenser's use of dialect forms is negligible after the *Calender*, for which it was appropriate. Yet dialect and archaism, which it is not always easy to separate due to the innate conservatism of dialect, converge in such words as 'afeared', 'noule', 'totty' (probably remembered from Chaucer's 'Reeve's Tale'), and 'stoures', which have Northern origins, as do such prepositions as 'fro' and 'til'. It is equally difficult to distinguish coinage from metaplasm. 'Astonied' seems metaplastic; 'tickle', in the sense of 'insecure', a variant meaning of a current word, but 'addoom', 'dewfull', 'obliquid', and 'Titanesse' are coinages. 'Hapless' and 'stage' are useful adaptations, the former among the slightly fewer than half of Spenser's innovations or revivals which have survived. 'Joyance', of which there are two instances in the *Cantos*, is a Spenserian hybrid in use as late as 1879 (*OED*). Similar in function to coinages are compounds, an aspect of Spenser's diction much imitated. Their intensifying rôle is best illustrated by 'off-scum', 'thunder-driue', 'Nectar-deawed', and 'levin-brond'—all in 7.6.30.

GRAMMAR AND SYNTAX

Spenser's grammar is as representative of the sixteenth century as Shakespeare's and—considering his aim and genre—properly more formal, learned, and self-conscious. The modern reader will note such characteristic Elizabethan 'errors' as disagreement of verb and subject (7.6.30.2), dangling participles (7.7.57.1), and the 'confusion' of *shall* and *will*. Certain constructions reinforce the effect of archaic diction. Among these are the omission of pronouns, especially as subjects (7.6.25.4; 7.7.12.1), the omission of articles (7.6.24.2) or prepositions (7.7.15.9), and such constructions as 'for to shroude' (7.6.39.2) and 'made . . . knowne to be' (7.6.40.6). There are also some recollections of Latin: the historical present in 7.6.49.3, the omission of the verb in 7.7.49.1, the

[1] J. Draper, 'Spenser's Use of the Perfective Prefix', *MLN* 48 (1933), 226–8, and Sugden, *op. cit.*, 11.

construction in 7.6.25.1, and the comparative in the sense of 'too' in the phrase 'my weaker wit' in 7.7.2.2. Archaic and Latinate effects, however, are more often matters of word order, especially of inversion.

But borrowing and innovation are only peripheral to the effect of the *Cantos*, as are Spenser's fondness for the non-restrictive clause over the restrictive, that is, for elaboration over definition, and his related emphasis on adjective and noun. Spenser's diction, metre and sound fuse to form a highly ceremonial language, abstracted from common speech as the Circle of the Moon and Faeryland are abstracted from the common condition. Its ceremonial character is continually exemplified in the minor architecture of phrase and line, in the balance of

> vaine errour or inducement light
> (7.6.32.2)

which leads straight to Milton, and in the cool symmetry of

> To bandie Crownes, and Kingdomes to bestowe
> (7.6.32.8)

which leads to Pope. One is continually aware of an almost spatial arrangement of the stanza: sound against sound, line against line, idea against idea (see 7.7.14, for example), despite which the narrative progresses, rarely descending to the arid exposition of 7.6.3. Accordingly, the most pervasive and important feature of the composition of the *Cantos* is their rhetoric.

RHETORIC

'Rhetoric', wrote the late editor of this series, 'is the greatest barrier between us and our ancestors', and 'we must reconcile ourselves to the fact that of the praise and censure which we allot to medieval and Elizabethan poets only the smallest part would have seemed relevant to those poets themselves'.[1] Rhetoric, now often 'mere' or 'empty' rhetoric, was in

[1] C. S. Lewis, *English Literature in the Sixteenth Century* (1954), p. 61.

Spenser's day inseparable from (or among the Ramists parallel to) logic as the foundation of style and eloquence, the vehicle of humane learning, and the chief qualification for public life. Spenser mastered its elements: *inventio* (the discovery of materials in reason or in the traditional *topoi* or commonplaces); *dispositio* (the composition of these materials), and *elocutio* (their expression through appropriate figurative language) at the Merchant Taylors' School, and he mastered them so well that fifty-one of the fifty-seven figures defined in Alexander Gil's *Logonomia Anglica* (1619, 1621) are illustrated from the poet's works. John Milton, studying under Gil at St Paul's, may have conned his tropes in snippets from *The Faerie Queene*.[1]

To discuss the rhetoric of the *Cantos* fully would be to annotate each line. It influences both the large aspects of organization and the figurative detail of the poem. Mutabilitie's speech is patterned on classical judicial oratory, whose principles were readily available in Cicero (Spenser may have used *De Inventione* directly) and Quintilian's *Institutes of Oratory*, which he certainly knew. Stanzas 14 and 15 constitute an *exordium* or beginning, 16 the *narratio*, stanzas 17–47 the *probatio* or proof, with the second line of 17 being a *propositio*. Lines 3–5 are a *partitio* or division of the material. In stanzas 49–55 Mutabilitie presents her *refutatio* or confutation, and in 56 her *peroratio* or conclusion. She employs the *topoi* of 'the whole and its parts' (17–26), and 'natural time' (27–46). Classical judicial oratory prescribes the flattering tone of stanzas 14 and 15 and Mutabilitie's affected modesty toward the court, as it does the syllogistic character of her presentation and Nature's reply. The primary interest of modern readers will lie in Spenser's *elocutio*, especially in his use of figurative language. Yet in the *Cantos*, as in his poetry generally, 'rhetorical schemes play a far greater part than the tropes, a fact which accounts for the intense and continuous formal

[1] See D. L. Clark, *John Milton at St. Paul's School* (1948), p. 74. Spenser was a favourite source of illustrations for other logical and rhetorical works, notably those of the Ramist Abraham Fraunce.

patterning that distinguishes his style from Shakespeare's.[1] In addition to figures already noted, one finds a wide variety used almost throughout the *Cantos*.

Veré Rubel[2] singles out the opening lines of 7.7.46 for attention, and her examination may be amplified, at the risk of an instructive weariness, as follows. The first few lines provide instances of *prosopopoeia* in the attribution of human qualities to Life and Death. The repetition of 'Death' in line 2 is an example of *anadiplosis*; 'grim and griesly' provide both an inoffensive *pleonasmus* and *alliteration*. The repetition of forms of 'seene' ('see', 'vnseene') is a *polyptoton*, and in its organization toward the climax of 'vnseene', it approaches a *gradatio*. Line three is an instance of *meiosis* or 'making little'. The description of Death is a variant of *peristasis* that leads to the *brachylogia* or 'cutted comma' of line five. The rest of the stanza, dealing with Life, provides examples of contrasting content but similar figurative use as in the *pleonasmus* of 'young' and 'boy', the *alliteration* of line 6 and the *polyptoton* moving from 'life' to 'lively' and kept in motion by 'like' and 'delightfull'.

One notes that Spenser here as elsewhere hazards such recognized 'vices of language' as *pleonasmus* and *barbarismus* (1.4), and that the strength of the stanza does not lie, as it does with Shakespeare, in metaphor, simile or in figures—nowadays considered centrally poetic—like *catachresis* (verb-adjective transfer), or *syllepsis* of the sense (application of one word in different contexts). The strength of the stanza lies in its architecture and musicality: in the contrast of the two parts of the stanza, the movement from 'seene' to 'vnseene', from 'Life' to 'lively'. To call Death a parting of the breath or like a shade, to compare Life to a young lusty boy or to a golden-winged Cupid seems—beside the metaphors and similes of Shakespeare—perfunctory and flat, the last quality emphasized by the almost anti-climatic phrase, 'fit to employ'. In these figures Spenser draws so heavily on commonplaces of image

[1] See H. D. Rix, *Rhetoric in Spenser's Poetry* (1940), p. 46.
[2] *Op. cit.*, 252. Convenient definitions may be found in an appendix.

and idea that they seem entirely lacking in the essential quality of metaphor, the perception of similarities in the dissimilar, through which poetry effects surprise and revelation. Spenser in this stanza gives us nothing of a phrase like Shakespeare's description of armour 'that scalds with safety', with its sensuous immediacy and its evocation of experiential or philosophical depths where the relation between danger and safety becomes ironic. Yet this is not to say his poetry lacks the depth one associates with metaphor. One must look for that in the whole, rather than in the smaller verbal strokes, of his work. The *Cantos*, as is the rest of *The Faerie Queene*, are an extended metaphor. Recognition of the poet's meaning comes not in shocks, as with the metaphors of Shakespeare, but gathers slowly as one perceives the common condition emerging from Diana's groves and the council of the gods. The figurative language of the *Cantos* may seem decorously tame. But Spenser's style flows from the nature of his attempt. One must recognize that the attempt often succeeded, and not wish our literature less rich by lamenting that Spenser was not Shakespeare.

THE TEXT

This edition is based on the Newberry Library (Chicago) copy of the 1609 folio edition of *The Faerie Queene*, the first to contain the *Cantos*. According to F. R. Johnson, there are 'a great many' copies of this edition in existence, testimony to its popularity, as are succeeding editions.[1] No manuscript of the *Cantos*, or, indeed, of any part of *The Faerie Queene* has been discovered despite apparently diligent searches from at least as early as the 1660s.[2] Later editions have no independent authority, and the 1609 text is followed with several corrections of obvious misprints indicated in the Notes.

[1] F. R. Johnson, *A Critical Bibliography of the Works of Edmund Spenser Printed before 1700* (1933), pp. 21–33; on Spenser's popularity see M. Eccles, 'A Survey of Elizabethan Readers', *Huntington Library Quarterly* 5 (1942), 180–2.

[2] J. Wurtsbaugh, *Two Centuries of Spenserian Scholarship* (1936), pp. 20–3.

The spelling of the 1609 edition is retained; it is neither unclear nor mannered, and modernization might result in a loss of richness, as would be the case, for example, if 'trauailers' in 6.9.9 had been altered to 'travelers'. The *Cantos* and indeed the whole of the 1609 edition appear to be more heavily punctuated than are earlier editions of the rest of *The Faerie Queene*. The punctuation is mechanical, with no apparent regard for rhythmical effects, and seems to be the work of compositors. In accordance with the practice of this series, both punctuation and capitalization have been modernized.

Two Cantos
of
Mvtabilitie

which, both for forme and matter, appeare
to be parcell of some following books of the

Faerie Queene

vnder the Legend
of
Constancie

CANTO VI

Proud Change (not pleasd in mortall things
    Beneath the moone to raigne)
Pretends, as well of gods as men,
    To be the soueraine.

I

What man that sees the euer-whirling wheele
  Of Change, the which all mortall things doth sway,
  But that therby doth find and plainly feele
  How Mvtability in them doth play
  Her cruell sports, to many men's decay?
  Which that to all may better yet appeare,
  I will rehearse that whylome I heard say,
  How she at first her selfe began to reare
Gainst all the gods, and th'empire sought from them to beare.

2

But first, here falleth fittest to vnfold
  Her antique race and linage ancient,
  As I haue found it registred of old
  In Faery Land mongst records permanent.
  She was, to weet, a daughter by descent
  Of those old Titans, that did whylome striue
  With Saturne's sonne for heauen's regiment;
  Whom though high Ioue of kingdome did depriue,
Yet many of their stemme long after did suruiue.

3

And many of them afterwards obtain'd
 Great power of Ioue, and high authority;
 As Hecaté, in whose almighty hand,
 He plac't all rule and principality,
 To be by her disposed diuersly
 To gods and men as she them list diuide;
 And drad Bellona, that doth sound on hie
 Warres and allarums vnto nations wide,
That makes both heauen and earth to tremble at her pride.

4

So likewise did this Titanesse aspire,
 Rule and dominion to her selfe to gaine,
 That as a goddesse men might her admire,
 And heauenly honours yield, as to them twaine.
 And first on earth she sought it to obtaine,
 Where she such proofe and sad examples shewed
 Of her great power, to many one's great paine,
 That not men onely (whom she soone subdewed)
But eke all other creatures her bad dooings rewed.

5

For she the face of earthly things so changed
 That all which Nature had establisht first
 In good estate, and in meet order ranged,
 She did pervert, and all their statutes burst.
 And all the world's faire frame (which none yet durst
 Of gods or men to alter or misguide)
 She alter'd quite, and made them all accurst
 That God had blest and did at first prouide
In that still happy state for euer to abide.

6

Ne shee the lawes of Nature onely brake,
　But eke of iustice and of policie,
　And wrong of right, and bad of good did make,
　And death for life exchanged foolishlie;
　Since which, all liuing wights haue learn'd to die,
　And all this world is woxen daily worse.
　O pittious worke of Mvtabilitie!
　By which we all are subiect to that curse,
And death in stead of life haue sucked from our nurse.

7

And now, when all the earth she thus had brought
　To her behest, and thralled to her might,
　She gan to cast in her ambitious thought
　T'attempt th'empire of the heauens' hight,
　And Ioue himselfe to shoulder from his right.
　And first she past the region of the ayre,
　And of the fire, whose substance thin and slight,
　Made no resistance, ne could her contraire,
But ready passage to her pleasure did prepaire.

8

Thence to the circle of the Moone she clambe,
　Where Cynthia raignes in euerlasting glory,
　To whose bright shining palace straight she came,
　All fairely deckt with heauen's goodly story;
　Whose siluer gates (by which there sate an hory
　Old aged sire, with hower-glasse in hand,
　Hight Tyme) she entred, were he liefe or sory;
　Ne staide till she the highest stage had scand,
Where Cynthia did sit, that neuer still did stand.

9

Her sitting on an iuory throne shee found,
　　Drawne of two steeds, th'one black, the other white,
　　Environd with tenne thousand starres around,
　　That duly her attended day and night;
　　And by her side there ran her page, that hight
　　Vesper, whom we the euening-starre intend,
　　That with his torche, still twinkling like twylight,
　　Her lightened all the way where she should wend,
And ioy to weary wandring trauailers did lend.

10

That when the hardy Titanesse beheld
　　The goodly building of her palace bright,
　　Made of the heauens' substance, and vp-held
　　With thousand crystall pillors of huge hight,
　　Shee gan to burne in her ambitious spright,
　　And t'envie her that in such glorie raigned.
　　Eftsoones she cast by force and tortious might
　　Her to displace, and to her selfe to haue gained
The kingdome of the night, and waters by her wained.

11

Boldly she bid the goddesse downe descend
　　And let her selfe into that ivory throne;
　　For shee her selfe more worthy thereof wend,
　　And better able it to guide alone.
　　Whether to men, whose fall she did bemone,
　　Or vnto gods, whose state she did maligne,
　　Or to th'infernall powers her need giue lone
　　Of her faire light, and bounty most benigne,
Her selfe of all that rule shee deemed most condigne.

12

But shee that had to her that soueraigne seat
  By highest Ioue assign'd, therein to beare
  Night's burning lamp, regarded not her threat,
  Ne yielded ought for fauour or for feare;
  But with sterne countenaunce and disdainfull cheare,
  Bending her horned browes, did put her back,
  And boldly blaming her for comming there,
  Bade her attonce from heauen's coast to pack,
Or at her perill bide the wrathfull thunder's wrack.

13

Yet nathemore the Giantesse forbare;
  But boldly preacing-on, raught forth her hand
  To pluck her downe perforce from off her chaire,
  And there-with lifting vp her golden wand,
  Threatned to strike her if she did with-stand.
  Where-at the starres, which round about her blazed,
  And eke the Moone's bright wagon still did stand,
  All beeing with so bold attempt amazed,
And on her vncouth habit and sterne looke still gazed.

14

Meane-while, the lower world, which nothing knew
  Of all that chaunced here, was darkned quite;
  And eke the heauens, and all the heauenly crew
  Of happy wights, now vnpurvaide of light,
  Were much afraid, and wondred at that sight,
  Fearing least Chaos broken had his chaine
  And brought againe on them eternall night.
  But chiefely Mercury, that next doth raigne,
Ran forth in haste vnto the king of gods to plaine.

15

All ran together with a great out-cry
   To Ioue's faire palace, fixt in heauen's hight,
   And beating at his gates full earnestly,
   Gan call to him aloud with all their might
   To know what meant that suddaine lack of light.
   The father of the gods, when this he heard,
   Was troubled much at their so strange affright,
   Doubting least Typhon were againe vprear'd,
Or other his old foes, that once him sorely fear'd.

16

Eftsoones the sonne of Maia forth he sent
   Downe to the circle of the Moone to knowe
   The cause of this so strange astonishment,
   And why shee did her wonted course forslowe;
   And if that any were on earth belowe
   That did with charmes or magick her molest,
   Him to attache, and downe to hell to throwe.
   But, if from heauen it were, then to arrest
The author and him bring before his presence prest.

17

The wingd-foot god so fast his plumes did beat,
   That soone he came where-as the Titanesse
   Was striuing with faire Cynthia for her seat;
   At whose strange sight and haughty hardinesse,
   He wondred much, and feared her no lesse.
   Yet laying feare aside to doe his charge,
   At last he bade her with bold stedfastnesse
   Ceasse to molest the Moone to walke at large,
Or come before high Ioue, her dooings to discharge.

18

And there-with-all he on her shoulder laid
   His snaky-wreathed mace, whose awfull power
   Doth make both gods and hellish fiends affraid.
   Where-at the Titanesse did sternely lower,
   And stoutly answer'd that in euill hower
   He from his Ioue such message to her brought,
   To bid her leaue faire Cynthia's siluer bower,
   Sith shee his Ioue and him esteemed nought,
No more then Cynthia's selfe, but all their kingdoms sought.

19

The heauens' herald staid not to reply,
   But past away, his doings to relate
   Vnto his lord, who now in th'highest sky,
   Was placed in his principall estate,
   With all the gods about him congregate.
   To whom when Hermes had his message told,
   It did them all exceedingly amate,
   Saue Ioue, who, changing nought his count'nance bold,
Did vnto them at length these speeches wise vnfold;

20

'Harken to mee awhile, yee heauenly powers.
   Ye may remember since th'Earth's cursed seed
   Sought to assaile the heauens' eternall towers,
   And to vs all exceeding feare did breed.
   But how we then defeated all their deed
   Yee all doe knowe, and them destroied quite;
   Yet not so quite, but that there did succeed
   An off-spring of their bloud, which did alite
Vpon the fruitfull earth, which doth vs yet despite.

21

'Of that bad seed is this bold woman bred
  That now with bold presumption doth aspire
  To thrust faire Phoebe from her siluer bed,
  And eke our selues from heauen's high empire,
  If that her might were match to her desire.
  Wherefore, it now behoues vs to advise
  What way is best to driue her to retire;
  Whether by open force, or counsell wise,
Areed, ye sonnes of God, as best ye can deuise.'

22

So hauing said, he ceast. And with his brow—
  His black eye-brow, whose doomefull dreaded beck
  Is wont to wield the world vnto his vow,
  And euen the highest Powers of heauen to check—
  Made signe to them in their degrees to speake;
  Who straight gan cast their counsell graue and wise.
  Meane-while th'Earth's daughter, thogh she nought did reck
  Of Hermes' message, yet gan now aduise
What course were best to take in this hot bold emprize.

23

Eftsoones she thus resolv'd: that whil'st the gods—
  After returne of Hermes' embassie—
  Were troubled, and amongst themselues at ods,
  Before they could new counsels re-allie,
  To set vpon them in that extasie,
  And take what fortune time and place would lend.
  So forth she rose, and through the purest sky
  To Ioue's high palace straight cast to ascend
To prosecute her plot. Good on-set boads good end.

24

Shee there arriuing, boldly in did pass;
 Where all the gods she found in counsell close,
 All quite vnarm'd, as then their manner was.
 At sight of her they suddaine all arose
 In great amaze, ne wist what way to chose.
 But Ioue, all fearelesse, forc't them to aby;
 And in his soueraine throne, gan straight dispose
 Himselfe more full of grace and maiestie,
That mote encheare his friends, and foes mote terrifie.

25

That, when the haughty Titanesse beheld,
 All were she fraught with pride and impudence,
 Yet with the sight thereof was almost queld;
 And inly quaking, seem'd as reft of sense
 And voyd of speech in that drad audience,
 Vntill that Ioue himselfe her selfe bespake:
 'Speake, thou fraile woman, speake with confidence,
 Whence art thou, and what doost thou here now make?
What idle errand hast thou, earth's mansion to forsake?'

26

Shee, halfe confused with his great commaund,
 Yet gathering spirit of her nature's pride,
 Him boldly answer'd thus to his demaund:
 'I am a daughter, by the mother's side,
 Of her that is grand-mother magnifide
 Of all the gods, great Earth, great Chaos' child.
 But by the father's (be it not envide)
 I greater am in bloud (whereon I build)
Then all the Gods, though wrongfully from heauen exil'd.

27

'For, Titan (as ye all acknowledge must)
  Was Saturne's elder brother by birth-right,
  Both sonnes of Vranus; but by vniust
  And guilefull meanes, through Corybantes' slight,
  The younger thrust the elder from his right;
  Since which, thou, Ioue, iniuriously hast held
  The heauens' rule from Titan's sonnes by might;
  And them to hellish dungeons downe hast feld.
Witness, ye heauens, the truth of all that I haue teld.'

28

Whil'st she thus spake, the gods, that gaue good eare
  To her bold words, and marked well her grace,
  Beeing of stature tall as any there
  Of all the gods, and beautifull of face
  As any of the goddesses in place,
  Stood all astonied, like a sort of steeres
  Mongst whom some beast of strange and forraine race
  Vnwares is chaunc't, far straying from his peeres.
So did their ghastly gaze bewray their hidden feares.

29

Till hauing pauz'd awhile, Ioue thus bespake:
  'Will neuer mortall thoughts ceasse to aspire
  In this bold sort to heauen claime to make,
  And touch celestiall seates with earthly mire?
  I would haue thought that bold Procrustes' hire,
  Or Typhon's fall, or proud Ixion's paine,
  Or great Prometheus, tasting of our ire,
  Would haue suffiz'd the rest for to restraine;
And warn'd all men by their example to refraine.

30

'But now this off-scum of that cursed fry
    Dare to renew the like bold enterprize,
    And chalenge th'heritage of this our skie;
    Whom what should hinder but that we likewise
    Should handle as the rest of her allies,
    And thunder-driue to hell?' With that, he shooke
    His nectar-deawed locks, with which the skyes
    And all the world beneath for terror quooke,
And eft his burning levin-brond in hand he tooke.

31

But when he looked on her louely face,
    In which faire beames of beauty did appeare
    That could the greatest wrath soone turne to grace
    (Such sway doth beauty euen in heauen beare),
    He staide his hand; and hauing chang'd his cheare,
    He thus againe in milder wise began:
    'But ah! if gods should striue with flesh yfere,
    Then shortly should the progeny of man
Be rooted out, if Ioue should doe still what he can.

32

'But thee, faire Titan's child, I rather weene,
    Through some vaine errour or inducement light
    To see that mortall eyes haue neuer seene;
    Or through ensample of thy sister's might,
    Bellona, whose great glory thou doost spight,
    Since thou hast seene her dreadfull power belowe
    Mongst wretched men, dismaide with her affright,
    To bandie crownes and kingdomes to bestowe—
And sure thy worth, no lesse then hers doth seem to showe.

7

33

'But wote thou this, thou hardy Titanesse,
  That not the worth of any liuing wight
  May challenge ought in heauen's interesse,
  Much lesse the title of old Titan's right.
  For we by conquest of our soueraine might,
  And by eternall doome of Fates' decree,
  Haue wonne the empire of the heauens bright;
  Which to our selues we hold, and to whom wee
Shall worthy deeme partakers of our blisse to bee.

34

'Then ceasse thy idle claime, thou foolish gerle,
  And seeke by grace and goodnesse to obtaine
  That place from which by folly Titan fell;
  There-to thou maist perhaps, if so thou faine,
  Haue Ioue thy gratious lord and soueraigne.'
  So, hauing said, she thus to him replide:
  'Ceasse, Saturne's sonne, to seeke by proffers vaine
  Of idle hopes t'allure mee to thy side,
For to betray my right before I haue it tride.

35

'But thee, O Ioue, no equall iudge I deeme
  Of my desert, or of my dewfull right,
  That in thine owne behalfe maist partiall seeme.
  But to the highest him, that is behight
  Father to gods and men by equall might,
  To weet, the god of nature, I appeale.'
  There-at Ioue wexed wroth, and in his spright
  Did inly grudge, yet did it well conceale,
And bade Dan Phoebus Scribe her appellation seale.

36

Eftsoones the time and place appointed were
   Where all, both heauenly powers and earthly wights,
   Before great Nature's presence should appeare
   For triall of their titles and best rights.
   That was, to weet, vpon the highest hights
   Of Arlo-Hill (Who knowes not Arlo-Hill?)
   That is the highest head, in all men's sights,
   Of my old father Mole, whom shepheard's quill
Renowmed hath with hymnes fit for a rurall skill.

37

And were it not ill fitting for this file,
   To sing of hilles and woods mongst warres and knights,
   I would abate the sternenesse of my stile,
   Mongst these sterne stounds to mingle soft delights,
   And tell how Arlo through Diana's spights
   (Beeing of old the best and fairest hill
   That was in all this holy-island's hights)
   Was made the most vnpleasant and most ill.
Meane while, O Clio, lend Calliope thy quill.

38

Whylome when Ireland florished in fame
   Of wealths and goodnesse, far aboue the rest
   Of all that beare the British Islands' name,
   The gods then vs'd, for pleasure and for rest,
   Oft to resort there-to, when seem'd them best.
   But none of all there-in more pleasure found
   Then Cynthia, that is soueraine queene profest
   Of woods and forrests, which therein abound,
Sprinkled with wholsom waters more then most on ground.

39

But mongst them all, as fittest for her game,
  Either for chace of beasts with hound or boawe,
  Or for to shroude in shade from Phoebus' flame,
  Or bathe in fountaines that doe freshly flowe
  Or from high hilles or from the dales belowe,
  She chose this Arlo; where shee did resort
  With all her nymphes enranged on a rowe,
  With whom the woody gods did oft consort;
For with the nymphes the satyres loue to play and sport.

40

Amongst the which, there was a nymph that hight
  Molanna, daughter of old father Mole,
  And sister vnto Mulla, faire and bright,
  Vnto whose bed false Bregog whylome stole,
  That shepheard Colin dearely did condole,
  And make her lucklesse loues well knowne to be.
  But this Molanna, were she not so shole,
  Were no lesse faire and beautifull then shee;
Yet as she is, a fairer flood may no man see.

41

For first she springs out of two marble rocks
  On which a groue of oakes high mounted growes,
  That as a girlond seemes to deck the locks
  Of som faire bride, brought forth with pompous showes
  Out of her bowre, that many flowers strowes;
  So through the flowry dales she, tumbling downe
  Through many woods and shady coverts, flowes,
  That on each side her siluer channell crowne,
Till to the plaine she come, whose valleyes shee doth drowne.

42

In her sweet streames, Diana vsed oft,
　　After her sweatie chace and toilesome play,
　　To bathe her selfe; and after, on the soft
　　And downy grasse, her dainty limbes to lay
　　In couert shade, where none behold her may,
　　For much she hated sight of liuing eye.
　　Foolish god Faunus, though full many a day
　　He saw her clad, yet longed foolishly
To see her naked mongst her nymphes in priuity.

43

No way he found to compasse his desire,
　　But to corrupt Molanna, this her maid,
　　Her to discouer for some secret hire.
　　So her with flattering words he first assaid;
　　And after, pleasing gifts for her purvaid,
　　Queene-apples and red cherries from the tree,
　　With which he her allured and betraid
　　To tell what time he might her lady see
When she her selfe did bathe, that he might secret bee.

44

There-to hee promist, if shee would him pleasure
　　With this small boone, to quit her with a better,
　　To weet, that where-as shee had out of measure
　　Long lov'd the Fanchin, who by nought did set her,
　　That he would vndertake, for this to get her
　　To be his loue, and of him liked well.
　　Besides all which, he vow'd to be her debter
　　For many moe good turnes then he would tell,
The least of which this little pleasure should excell.

45

The simple maid did yield to him anone,
   And eft him placed where he close might view
   That neuer any saw, saue onely one;
   Who, for his hire to so foole-hardy dew,
   Was of his hounds devour'd in hunter's hew.
   Tho, as her manner was on sunny day,
   Diana, with her nymphes about her, drew
   To this sweet spring; where, doffing her array,
She bath'd her louely limbes, for Ioue a likely pray.

46

There Faunus saw that pleased much his eye,
   And made his hart to tickle in his brest;
   That for great ioy of some-what he did spy
   He could him not containe in silent rest,
   But breaking forth in laughter, loud profest
   His foolish thought. A foolish faune indeed,
   That couldst not hold thy selfe, so hidden, blest,
   But wouldest needs thine owne conceit areed!
Babblers vnworthy been of so diuine a meed.

47

The goddesse, all abashed with that noise,
   In haste forth started from the guilty brooke;
   And running straight where-as she heard his voice,
   Enclos'd the bush about, and there him tooke
   Like darred larke, not daring vp to looke
   On her whose sight before so much he sought.
   Thence forth they drew him by the hornes, and shooke
   Nigh all to peeces, that they left him nought;
And then into the open light they forth him brought.

48

Like as an huswife, that with busie care
  Thinks of her dairie to make wondrous gaine,
  Finding where-as some wicked beast vnware
  That breakes into her dayr'house there doth draine
  Her creaming pannes, and frustrate all her paine,
  Hath, in some snare or gin set close behind,
  Entrapped him, and caught into her traine,
  Then thinkes what punishment were best assign'd,
And thousand deathes deuiseth in her vengefull mind—

49

So did Diana and her maydens all
  Vse silly Faunus, now within their baile.
  They mocke and scorne him, and him foule miscall;
  Some by the nose him pluckt, some by the taile,
  And by his goatish beard some did him haile.
  Yet he (poore soule) with patience all did beare,
  For nought against their wils might countervaile;
  Ne ought he said what euer he did heare,
But hanging downe his head, did like a mome appeare.

50

At length, when they had flouted him their fill,
  They gan to cast what penaunce him to giue.
  Some would haue gelt him, but that same would spill
  The wood-god's breed, which must for euer liue;
  Others would through the riuer him haue driue,
  And ducked deepe, but that seem'd penaunce light.
  But most agreed, and did this sentence giue,
  Him in deare's skin to clad, and in that plight,
To hunt him with their hounds, him selfe saue how hee might.

51

But Cynthia's selfe, more angry than the rest,
   Thought not enough to punish him in sport,
   And of her shame to make a gamesome iest,
   But gan examine him in straighter sort,
   Which of her nymphes or other close consort
   Him thither brought and her to him betraid?
   He, much affeard, to her confessed short
   That 'twas Molanna which her so bewraid.
Then all attonce their hands vpon Molanna laid.

52

But him, according as they had decreed,
   With a deere's-skin they couered, and then chast
   With all their hounds that after him did speed;
   But he, more speedy, from them fled more fast
   Then any deere, so sore him dread aghast.
   They after follow'd all with shrill out-cry,
   Shouting as they the heauens would haue brast,
   That all the woods and dales where he did flie
Did ring againe, and loud reeccho to the skie.

53

So they him follow'd till they weary were.
   When back returning to Molann' againe,
   They, by commaund'ment of Diana, there
   Her whelm'd with stones. Yet Faunus, for her paine,
   Of her beloued Fanchin did obtaine
   That her he would receiue vnto his bed.
   So now her waues passe through a pleasant plaine
   Till with the Fanchin she her selfe doe wed,
And, both combin'd, themselues in one faire riuer spred.

54

Nath'lesse Diana, full of indignation,
   Thence-forth abandoned her delicious brooke,
   In whose sweet streame, before that bad occasion,
   So much delight to bathe her limbes she tooke.
   Ne onely her, but also quite forsooke
   All those faire forrests about Arlo hid,
   And all that mountaine, which doth over-looke
   The richest champian that may else be rid,
And the faire Shure, in which are thousand salmons bred.

55

Them all, and all that she so deare did way,
   Thence-forth she left; and parting from the place,
   There-on an heauy haplesse curse did lay:
   To weet, that wolues where she was wont to space
   Should harbour'd be, and all those woods deface,
   And thieues should rob and spoile that coast around.
   Since which those woods and all that goodly chase
   Doth to this day with wolues and thieues abound;
Which too-too true that land's in-dwellers since haue found.

CANTO VII

Pealing from Ioue to Natur's bar,
   Bold Alteration pleades
Large euidence, but Nature soone
   Her righteous doome areads.

1

Ah! whither doost thou now, thou greater Muse
   Me from these woods and pleasing forrests bring?
   And my fraile spirit—that dooth oft refuse
   This too high flight, vnfit for her weake wing—
   Lift vp aloft, to tell of heauen's king
   (Thy soueraine sire) his fortunate successe,
   And victory in bigger noates to sing,
   Which he obtain'd against that Titanesse,
That him of heauen's empire sought to dispossesse.

2

Yet sith I needs must follow thy behest,
   Doe thou my weaker wit with skill inspire
   Fit for this turne; and in my feeble brest
   Kindle fresh sparks of that immortall fire
   Which learned minds inflameth with desire
   Of heauenly things. For who but thou alone,
   That art yborne of heauen and heauenly sire,
   Can tell things doen in heauen so long ygone,
So farre past memory of man that may be knowne.

3

Now at the time that was before agreed,
   The gods assembled all on Arlo Hill,
   As well those that are sprung of heauenly seed
   As those that all the other world doe fill,
   And rule both sea and land vnto their will.
   Onely th'infernall powers might not appeare,
   Aswell for horror of their count'naunce ill
   As for th'vnruly fiends which they did feare;
Yet Pluto and Proserpina were present there.

4

And thither also came all other creatures,
   What-euer life or motion doe retaine,
   According to their sundry kinds of features,
   That Arlo scarsly could them all containe,
   So full they filled euery hill and plaine.
   And had not Nature's Sergeant, that is Order,
   Them well disposed by his busie paine,
   And raunged farre abroad in euery border,
They would haue caused much confusion and disorder.

5

Then forth issewed—great goddesse—great Dame Nature
   With goodly port and gracious Maiesty,
   Being far greater and more tall of stature
   Then any of the gods or powers on hie.
   Yet certes by her face and physnomy,
   Whether she man or woman inly were,
   That could not any creature well descry;
   For with a veile that wimpled euery where,
Her head and face was hid, that mote to none appeare.

6

That, some doe say, was so by skill deuized
  To hide the terror of her vncouth hew
  From mortall eyes, that should be sore agrized,
  For that her face did like a lion shew,
  That eye of wight could not indure to view.
  But others tell that it so beautious was,
  And round about such beames of splendor threw,
  That it the sunne a thousand times did pass,
Ne could be seene but like an image in a glass.

7

That well may seemen true. For well I weene
  That this same day, when she on Arlo sat,
  Her garment was so bright and wondrous sheene
  That my fraile wit cannot deuize to what
  It to compare, nor finde like stuffe to that.
  As those three sacred saints, though else most wise,
  Yet on mount Thabor quite their wits forgat
  When they their glorious Lord in strange disguise
Transfigur'd sawe; his garments so did daze their eyes.

8

In a fayre plaine vpon an equall hill
  She placed was in a pauilion;
  Not such as craftes-men by their idle skill
  Are wont for princes' states to fashion;
  But th'Earth her self, of her owne motion,
  Out of her fruitfull bosome made to growe
  Most dainty trees, that shooting vp anon,
  Did seeme to bow their blossming heads full lowe,
For homage vnto her, and like a throne did shew.

9

So hard it is for any liuing wight
  All her array and vestiments to tell
  That old Dan Geffrey, in whose gentle spright
  The pure well head of Poesie did dwell,
  In his *Foules' Parley* durst not with it mel,
  But it transferd to Alane, who he thought
  Had in his *Plaint of Kindes* describ'd it well.
  Which who will read set forth so as it ought,
Go seek he out that Alane where he may be sought.

10

And all the earth for vnderneath her feete
  Was dight with flowres, that voluntary grew
  Out of the ground, and sent forth odours sweet—
  Tenne thousand mores of sundry sent and hew,
  That might delight the smell, or please the view—
  The which the nymphes from all the brooks thereby
  Had gathered, which they at her foot-stoole threw,
  That richer seem'd then any tapestry
That princes' bowres adorne with painted imagery.

11

And Mole himselfe, to honour her the more,
  Did deck himself in freshest faire attire;
  And his high head, that seemeth alwaies hore
  With hardned frosts of former winters' ire,
  He with an oaken girlond now did tire,
  As if the loue of some new nymph late seene
  Had in him kindled youthfull fresh desire,
  And made him change his gray attire to greene.
Ah gentle Mole! such ioyance hath thee well beseene.

12

Was neuer so great ioyance since the day
   That all the gods whylome assembled were
   On Haemus Hill in their diuine array
   To celebrate the solemne bridall cheare
   Twixt Peleus and dame Thetis pointed there;
   Where Phoebus' self, that god of poets hight,
   They say, did sing the spousall hymne full cleere,
   That all the gods were rauisht with delight
Of his celestiall song, and musick's wondrous might.

13

This great grandmother of all creatures bred,
   Great Nature, euer young yet full of eld,
   Still moouing, yet vnmoued from her sted;
   Vnseene of any, yet of all beheld;
   Thus sitting in her throne, as I haue teld—
   Before her came dame Mutabilitie,
   And being lowe before her presence feld,
   With meek obaysance and humilitie,
Thus gan her plaintif plea, with words to amplifie:

14

'To thee, O greatest goddesse, onely great,
   An humble suppliant, loe, I lowely fly,
   Seeking for right, which I of thee entreat,
   Who Right to all dost deale indifferently,
   Damning all wrong and tortious iniurie
   Which any of thy creatures doe to other,
   Oppressing them with power, vnequally,
   Sith of them all thou art the equall mother,
And knittest each to each, as brother vnto brother.

15

'To thee therefore of this same Ioue I plaine,
  And of his fellow gods that faine to be,
  That challenge to themselues the whole world's raign,
  Of which the greatest part is due to me,
  And heauen it selfe by heritage in fee.
  For heauen and earth I both alike do deeme,
  Sith heauen and earth are both alike to thee;
  And gods no more then men thou doest esteeme,
For euen the gods to thee, as men to gods do seeme.

16

'Then weigh, O soueraigne goddesse, by what right
  These gods do claime the world's whole souerainty,
  And that is onely dew vnto thy might
  Arrogate to themselues ambitiously.
  As for the gods' owne principality,
  Which Ioue vsurpes vniustly; that to be
  My heritage Ioue's self cannot deny,
  From my great grandsire Titan vnto mee,
Deriv'd by dew descent, as is well knowen to thee.

17

'Yet mauger Ioue and all his gods beside,
  I doe possesse the world's most regiment,
  As, if ye please it into parts diuide
  And euery part's inholders to conuent,
  Shall to your eyes appeare incontinent.
  And first, the Earth, great mother of vs all,
  That only seems vnmov'd and permanent
  And vnto Mutability not thrall,
Yet is she chang'd in part, and eeke in generall.

18

'For all that from her springs and is ybredde,
  How-euer fayre it flourish for a time,
  Yet see we soone decay, and, being dead,
  To turne again vnto their earthly slime.
  Yet out of their decay and mortall crime
  We daily see new creatures to arize,
  And of their winter spring another prime,
  Vnlike in forme and chang'd by strange disguise.
So turne they still about, and change in restlesse wise.

19

'As for her tenants, that is, man and beasts,
  The beasts we daily see massacred dy
  As thralls and vassals vnto men's beheasts.
  And men themselues doe change continually
  From youth to eld, from wealth to pouerty,
  From good to bad, from bad to worst of all.
  Ne doe their bodies only flit and fly;
  But eeke their minds, which they immortall call,
Still change and vary thoughts as new occasions fall.

20

'Ne is the water in more constant case,
  Whether those same on high or these belowe.
  For th'ocean moueth stil from place to place,
  And euery riuer still doth ebbe and flowe;
  Ne any lake that seems most still and slowe,
  Ne poole so small, that can his smoothnesse holde
  When any winde doth vnder heauen blowe;
  With which the clouds are also tost and roll'd,
Now like great hills, and streight like sluces them vnfold.

21

'So likewise are all watry liuing wights
   Still tost and turned with continuall change,
   Neuer abyding in their stedfast plights.
   The fish, still floting, doe at randon range
   And neuer rest, but euermore exchange
   Their dwelling places as the streames them carrie.
   Ne haue the watry foules a certaine grange
   Wherein to rest, ne in one stead do tarry,
But flitting still doe flie, and still their places vary.

22

'Next is the ayre; which who feeles not by sense
   (For of all sense it is the middle meane)
   To flit still, and with subtill influence
   Of his thin spirit, all creatures to maintaine
   In state of life? O weake life, that does leane
   On thing so tickle as th'vnsteady ayre,
   Which euery howre is chang'd and altred cleane
   With euery blast that bloweth fowle or faire.
The faire doth it prolong; the fowle doth it impaire.

23

'Therein the changes infinite beholde
   Which to her creatures euery minute chaunce;
   Now boyling hot, streight friezing deadly cold;
   Now faire sun-shine, that makes all skip and daunce;
   Streight, bitter storms and balefull countenance,
   That makes them all to shiuer and to shake.
   Rayne, hayle, and snowe do pay them sad penance,
   And dreadfull thunder-claps that make them quake,
With flames and flashing lights that thousand changes make

8

24

'Last is the fire; which though it liue for euer
  Ne can be quenched quite, yet euery day
  Wee see his parts, so soone as they do seuer,
  To lose their heat and shortly to decay—
  So makes himself his owne consuming pray.
  Ne any liuing creatures doth he breed,
  But all that are of others bredd doth slay,
  And with their death his cruell life dooth feed,
Nought leauing but their barren ashes, without seede.

25

'Thus all these fower, the which the ground-work bee
  Of all the world and of all liuing wights,
  To thousand sorts of change we subiect see.
  Yet are they chang'd by other wondrous slights
  Into themselues, and lose their natiue mights:
  The fire to aire, and th'ayre to water sheere,
  And water into earth. Yet water fights
  With fire, and aire with earth, approaching neere;
Yet all are in one body, and as one appeare.

26

'So in them all raignes Mutabilitie,
  How-euer these, that gods themselues do call,
  Of them doe claime the rule and souerainty:
  As Vesta of the fire aethereall,
  Vulcan of this, with vs so vsuall,
  Ops of the earth, and Iuno of the ayre,
  Neptune of seas, and nymphes of riuers all.
  For all those riuers to me subiect are,
And all the rest, which they vsurp, be all my share.

27

'Which to approuen true, as I haue told,
　Vouchsafe, O goddesse, to thy presence call
　The rest which doe the world in being hold,
　As times and seasons of the yeare that fall.
　Of all the which demand in generall,
　Or iudge thy selfe by verdit of thine eye,
　Whether to me they are not subiect all.'
　Nature did yeeld thereto, and by-and-by,
Bade Order call them all before her maiesty.

28

So forth issew'd the seasons of the yeare:
　First, lusty Spring, all dight in leaues of flowres
　That freshly budded and new bloosmes did beare,
　In which a thousand birds had built their bowres,
　That sweetly sung, to call forth paramours.
　And in his hand a iauelin he did beare;
　And on his head, as fit for warlike stoures,
　A guilt engrauen morion he did weare,
That as some did him loue, so others did him feare.

29

Then came the iolly Sommer, being dight
　In a thin silken cassock coloured greene,
　That was vnlyned all, to be more light.
　And on his head a girlond well beseene
　He wore, from which as he had chauffed been,
　The sweat did drop; and in his hand he bore
　A boawe and shaftes, as he in forrest greene
　Had hunted late the libbard or the bore,
And now would bathe his limbes, with labor heated sore.

30

Then came the Autumne all in yellow clad,
　　As though he ioyed in his plentious store,
　　Laden with fruits that made him laugh, full glad
　　That he had banisht hunger, which to-fore
　　Had by the belly oft him pinched sore.
　　Vpon his head a wreath that was enrold
　　With eares of corne of euery sort he bore;
　　And in his hand a sickle he did holde
To reape the ripened fruits the which the earth had yold.

31

Lastly came Winter cloathed all in frize,
　　Chattering his teeth for cold that did him chill,
　　Whil'st on his hoary beard his breath did freese,
　　And the dull drops that from his purpled bill
　　As from a limbeck did adown distill.
　　In his right hand a tipped staffe he held,
　　With which his feeble steps he stayed still;
　　For he was faint with cold and weak with eld,
That scarse his loosed limbes he hable was to weld.

32

These, marching softly, thus in order went,
　　And after them the monthes all riding came:
　　First, sturdy March, with brows full sternly bent,
　　And armed strongly, rode vpon a ram—
　　The same which ouer Hellespontus swam.
　　Yet in his hand a spade he also hent,
　　And in a bag all sorts of seeds ysame,
　　Which on the earth he strowed as he went,
And fild her womb with fruitfull hope of nourishment.

33

Next came fresh Aprill, full of lustyhed,
    And wanton as a kid whose horne new buds.
    Vpon a bull he rode, the same which led
    Europa floting through th'Argolick fluds.
    His hornes were gilden all with golden studs,
    And garnished with garlonds goodly dight
    Of all the fairest flowres and freshest buds
    Which th'earth brings forth, and wet he seem'd in sight
With wauues, through which he waded for his loue's delight.

34

Then came faire May, the fayrest mayd on ground,
    Deckt all with dainties of her season's pryde,
    And throwing flowres out of her lap around.
    Vpon two brethren's shoulders she did ride,
    The twinnes of Leda, which on eyther side
    Supported her like to their soueraine queene.
    Lord, how all creatures laught when her they spide,
    And leapt and daunc't as they had rauisht beene!
And Cupid selfe about her fluttred all in greene.

35

And after her came iolly Iune, arrayd
    All in greene leaues, as he a player were;
    Yet in his time he wrought as well as playd,
    That by his plough-yrons mote right well appeare.
    Vpon a crab he rode, that him did beare
    With crooked crawling steps an vncouth pase,
    And backward yode, as bargemen wont to fare,
    Bending their force contrary to their face,
Like that vngracious crew which faines demurest grace.

36

Then came hot Iuly, boyling like to fire,
   That all his garments he had cast away.
   Vpon a lyon raging yet with ire
   He boldly rode, and made him to obay.
   It was the beast that whylome did forray
   The Nemaean forrest, till th'Amphytrionide
   Him slew, and with his hide did him array.
   Behinde his back a sithe, and by his side
Vnder his belt he bore a sickle circling wide.

37

The sixt was August, being rich arrayd
   In garment all of gold downe to the ground.
   Yet rode he not, but led a louely mayd
   Forth by the lilly hand, the which was cround
   With eares of corne, and full her hand was found.
   That was the righteous virgin, which of old
   Liv'd here on earth, and plenty made abound;
   But after wrong was lov'd and iustice solde,
She left th'vnrighteous world and was to heauen extold.

38

Next him, September marched eeke on foote;
   Yet was he heauy laden with the spoyle
   Of haruests' riches, which he made his boot,
   And him enricht with bounty of the soyle.
   In his one hand, as fit for haruest's toyle,
   He held a knife-hook; and in th'other hand
   A paire of waights, with which he did assoyle
   Both more and lesse, where it in doubt did stand,
And equall gaue to each as iustice duly scann'd.

39

Then came October, full of merry glee.
  For yet his noule was totty of the must
  Which he was treading in the wine-fat's see,
  And of the ioyous oyle, whose gentle gust
  Made him so frollick and so full of lust.
  Vpon a dreadull scorpion he did ride,
  The same which by Diana's doom vniust
  Slew great Orion; and eeke by his side
He had his ploughing share and coulter ready tyde.

40

Next was Nouember, he full grosse and fat,
  As fed with lard, and that right well might seeme,
  For he had been a fatting hogs of late,
  That yet his browes with sweat did reek and steem;
  And yet the season was full sharp and breem.
  In planting eeke he took no small delight.
  Whereon he rode, not easie was to deeme;
  For it a dreadfull centaure was in sight,
The seed of Saturne and faire Nais, Chiron hight.

41

And after him came next the chill December.
  Yet he, through merry feasting which he made,
  And great bonfires, did not the cold remember—
  His Sauiour's birth his mind so much did glad.
  Vpon a shaggy-bearded goat he rade,
  The same wherewith Dan Ioue in tender yeares,
  They say, was nourisht by th'Idaean mayd.
  And in his hand a broad deepe boawle he beares,
Of which he freely drinks an health to all his peeres.

42

Then came old Ianuary, wrapped well
   In many weeds to keep the cold away;
   Yet did he quake and quiuer like to quell,
   And blowe his nayles to warme them if he may,
   For they were numbd with holding all the day
   An hatchet keene, with which he felled wood
   And from the trees did lop the needlesse spray.
   Vpon an huge great earth-pot steane he stood,
From whose wide mouth there flowed forth the Romane floud.

43

And lastly came cold February, sitting
   In an old wagon, for he could not ride,
   Drawne of two fishes for the season fitting,
   Which through the flood before did softly slyde
   And swim away. Yet had he by his side
   His plough and harnesse fit to till the ground,
   And tooles to prune the trees, before the pride
   Of hasting prime did make them burgein round.
So past the twelue months forth, and their dew places found.

44

And after these there came the Day and Night,
   Riding together both with equall pase,
   Th'one on a palfrey blacke, the other white.
   But Night had couered her vncomely face
   With a blacke veile, and held in hand a mace
   On top whereof the moon and stars were pight,
   And sleep and darknesse round about did trace.
   But Day did beare vpon his scepter's hight
The goodly sun, encompast all with beames bright.

45

Then came the Howres, faire daughters of high Ioue,
  And timely Night, the which were all endewed
  With wondrous beauty fit to kindle loue;
  But they were virgins all, and loue eschewed,
  That might forslack the charge of them fore-shewed
  By mighty Ioue, who did them porters make
  Of heauen's gate, whence all the gods issued,
  Which they did dayly watch, and nightly wake
By euen turnes, ne euer did their charge forsake.

46

And after all came Life, and lastly Death—
  Death with most grim and griesly visage seene.
  Yet is he nought but parting of the breath,
  Ne ought to see, but like a shade to weene,
  Vnbodied, vnsoul'd, vnheard, vnseene.
  But Life was like a faire young lusty boy,
  Such as they faine Dan Cupid to haue beene,
  Full of delightfull health and liuely ioy,
Deckt all with flowres, and wings of gold fit to employ.

47

When these were past, thus gan the Titanesse;
  'Lo, mighty mother, now be iudge and say
  Whether in all thy creatures more or lesse
  Change doth not raign and beare the greatest sway.
  For who sees not that time on all doth pray?
  But times do change and moue continually,
  So nothing here long standeth in one stay.
  Wherefore this lower world who can deny
But to be subiect still to Mutabilitie?'

48

Then thus gan Ioue: 'Right true it is that these
   And all things else that vnder heauen dwell
   Are chaung'd of time, who doth them all disseise
   Of being. But who is it, to me tell,
   That time himselfe doth moue and still compell
   To keepe his course? Is not that namely wee,
   Which poure that vertue from our heauenly cell
   That moues them all, and makes them changed be?
So them we gods doe rule, and in them also thee.'

49

To whom, thus Mutability: 'The things
   Which we see not how they are mov'd and swayd
   Ye may attribute to your selues as kings,
   And say they by your secret powre are made.
   But what we see not, who shall vs perswade?
   But were they so, as ye them faine to be,
   Mov'd by your might, and ordred by your ayde,
   Yet what if I can proue that euen yee
Your selues are likewise chang'd, and subiect vnto mee?

50

'And first, concerning her that is the first,
   Euen you, faire Cynthia, whom so much ye make
   Ioue's dearest darling, she was bred and nurst
   On Cynthus Hill, whence she her name did take.
   Then is she mortall borne, how-so ye crake.
   Besides, her face and countenance euery day
   We changed see, and sundry forms partake,
Now hornd, now round, now bright, now brown and gray;
So that "as changefull as the moone" men vse to say.

51

'Next Mercury, who though he lesse appeare
  To change his hew, and always seeme as one,
  Yet he his course doth altar euery yeare,
  And is of late far out of order gone.
  So Venus eeke, that goodly paragone,
  Though faire all night, yet is she darke all day;
  And Phoebus' self, who lightsome is alone,
  Yet is he oft eclipsed by the way,
And fills the darkned world with terror and dismay.

52

'Now Mars, that valiant man, is changed most.
  For he some times so far runs out of square,
  That he his way doth seem quite to haue lost,
  And cleane without his vsuall sphere to fare,
  That euen these star-gazers stonisht are
  At sight thereof, and damne their lying bookes.
  So likewise grim Sir Saturne oft doth spare
  His sterne aspect, and calme his crabbed lookes.
So many turning cranks these haue, so many crookes.

53

'But you, Dan Ioue, that only constant are,
  And king of all the rest, as ye do clame,
  Are you not subiect eeke to this misfare?
  Then let me aske you this withouten blame:
  Where were ye borne? Some say in Crete by name,
  Others in Thebes, and others other-where.
  But wheresoeuer, they comment the same:
  They all consent that ye begotten were
And borne here in this world, ne other can appeare.

54

'Then are ye mortall borne, and thrall to me,
  Vnlesse the kingdome of the sky yee make
  Immortall, and vnchangeable to be.
  Besides, that power and vertue which ye spake,
  That ye here worke, doth many changes take,
  And your owne natures change. For each of you
  That vertue haue or this or that to make,
  Is checkt and changed from his nature trew
By others' opposition or obliquid view.

55

'Besides, the sundry motions of your spheares,
  So sundry waies and fashions as clerkes faine,
  Some in short space, and some in longer yeares—
  What is the same but alteration plaine?
  Onely the starrie skie doth still remaine;
  Yet do the starres and signes therein still moue,
  And euen it self is mov'd, as wizards saine.
  But all that moueth, doth mutation loue;
Therefore both you and them to me I subiect proue.

56

Then since within this wide great vniuerse
  Nothing doth firme and permanent appeare,
  But all things tost and turned by transuerse,
  What then should let but I aloft should reare
  My trophee, and from all the triumph beare?
  Now iudge then, O thou greatest goddesse trew,
  According as thy selfe doest see and heare,
  And vnto me addoom that is my dew;
That is the rule of all, all being rul'd by you.'

57

So hauing ended, silence long ensewed;
  Ne Nature to or fro spake for a space,
  But with firme eyes affixt, the ground still viewed.
  Meane while all creatures, looking in her face,
  Expecting th'end of this so doubtfull case,
  Did hang in long suspence what would ensew,
  To whether side should fall the soueraigne place.
  At length, she looking vp with chearefull view,
The silence brake, and gaue her doome in speeches few.

58

'I well consider all that ye haue sayd,
  And find that all things stedfastnes doe hate,
  And changed be. Yet, being rightly wayd,
  They are not changed from their first estate,
  But by their change their being doe dilate,
  And turning to themselues at length againe,
  Doe worke their owne perfection so by fate.
  Then ouer them Change doth not rule and raigne;
But they raigne ouer Change, and doe their states maintaine.

59

'Cease therefore, daughter, further to aspire,
  And thee content thus to be rul'd by me;
  For thy decay thou seekst by thy desire.
  But time shall come that all shall changed bee,
  And from thenceforth none no more change shall see.'
  So was the Titaness put downe and whist,
  And Ioue confirm'd in his imperiall see.
  Then was that whole assembly quite dismist,
And Natur's selfe did vanish, whither no man wist.

THE VIII CANTO. VNPERFITE

1

When I bethinke me on that speech whyleare
   Of Mutability, and well it way,
   Me seemes that though she all vnworthy were
   Of the heav'n's rule, yet very sooth to say,
   In all things else she beares the greatest sway.
   Which makes me loath this state of life so tickle,
   And loue of things so vaine to cast away;
   Whose flowring pride, so fading and so fickle,
Short time shall soon cut down with his consuming sickle.

2

Then gin I thinke on that which Nature sayd,
   Of that same time when no more change shall be,
   But stedfast rest of all things firmely stayd
   Vpon the pillours of eternity,
   That is contrayr to mutabilitie.
   For all that moueth doth in change delight;
   But thence-forth all shall rest eternally
   With Him that is the God of Sabbaoth hight.
O that great Sabbaoth God, graunt me that Sabaoth's sight.

NOTES

All words or constructions likely to raise difficulties for the
modern reader are glossed at their first appearance.

CANTO VI

Proem. 1. Change. Another name for Mutabilitie. The transitoriness
of sublunary things after the Fall was a commonplace of Elizabethan
cosmology and social thought. See E. M. W. Tillyard, *Elizabethan
World Picture* (1944), p. 50, and Spenser's *Virgil's Gnat*, 544, for
example.

2. Pretends, 'attempts'.

1.2. The traditional image of Fortune's wheel appears in *FQ* 5.10.20.7,
and elsewhere in Spenser. The image, and the subject, are treated at
length in Patch, *The Goddess Fortuna* (1927).

6. Which that. A usage common in Chaucer, rare in the Elizabethans.
See Abbott, *A Shakespearian Grammar* (1909), p. 171.

7. whylome, 'formerly, once'. An archaism which Spenser uses
several times in the *Cantos*.

9. empire. The accent falls heavily on the first syllable, in part
because of the tendency of the alexandrine to break in half. Elsewhere
Spenser accents the word on the second syllable, as in Canto VI.21.4.
The shifting of accent for metrical purposes was recognized, though
uneasily, as permissible. See Puttenham, *Arte of English Poesie*, ed.
Willcock and Walker (1936), p. 162.

2.2. linage, 'lineage'. The figure of peristasis (description of ancestry),
was an almost obligatory topos of classical legal presentation;
Mutabilitie's ancestry plays an important part in the trial to follow.

4. At several other points Spenser refers casually to the records of
Faery, as in *FQ* 4.11.8. In 2.9.56ff. he includes historical and Faery
records in Eumnestes' collection.

5. to weet, 'to wit'. Spenser probably depended on the versions of the
myth of the Titans found in classical dictionaries such as those of
Comes and Stephanus. See H. Lotspeich, *Classical Mythology in the
Poetry of Edmund Spenser* (1932), pp. 111–12, and Starnes and Talbert,
Classical Myth and Legend in Renaissance Dictionaries (1955), p. 77.
The major classical telling of the Titan myth is in Hesiod, *Theog.* 207.

7. Saturne's sonne, 'Jove'. **regiment,** 'rule'.

3.3. Hecate is the infernal member of a triple deity—on earth Diana,
in heaven Luna. Spenser seems to depend on Comes 3.15 here,
although Hesiod, *Theog.* 411–52, describes Zeus as honouring her
with gifts and power.

4. **principality.** Possibly a glancing reference to the lowest of the three hierarchies of angels (fallen or unfallen) on the system of Pseudo-Dionysius. See Ephesians 6.12. R. West, *Milton and the Angels* (1955), p. 51, shows that Spenser used the Dionysian hierarchies in the Protestant manner, that is, vaguely. See also note to canto VII.3.6 below.

6. **list,** 'wished to'.

7. **drad,** 'dread'. **Bellona** is variously the daughter or sister, but most significantly the wife, of Mars, as in Shakespeare's depiction of Macbeth as 'Bellona's bridegroom', *Macbeth* 2.2.55. Lotspeich, p. 52, thinks Spenser's unclassical conception of Bellona as a Titan results from his recollection of his own translation of the *Visions of Bellay*, 15, where she seems to be identified with 'Typhaeus' sister', and, like Mutabilitie, 'Over all the world, did raise a trophee hie'.

9. **makes . . . to tremble.** An archaic construction, also found in 40.6 and Canto VII.23.6.

4.1. **Titanesse,** a coinage. Mutabilitie's aspirations are similar to those of Lucifera in *FQ* 1.4.11–12, though Mutabilitie, unlike Lucifera, is unwilling to rule by 'policie'—a significant point for her character.

3. **admire,** 'wonder at'.

4. **twain.** Hecate and Bellona.

7. **many one's.** An obsolescent form, not found in Shakespeare, for example.

5.1. Change, often thought of as the result of the Fall and thus presented here, was rarely viewed in Spenser's day as 'progress'. Yet later in the *Cantos*, in the pageant of the months for example, an evolutionary process is suggested, see Introd., 'Iconography'.

1. **Ne,** 'and not', current in Elizabethan English.

6.2. **eke,** 'also'. **Policie,** 'prudent government', but also 'cunning' and 'reason of state'.

4. The complex relation of Mutabilitie to the Fall is discussed in Introd., 'Mutabilitie'. 5.6. seems to make her work anterior to the Fall, and 6.3ff. a cause of it. Yet mere change would not recommend itself as the sufficient cause of the Fall on any orthodox view. Thus Spenser has it both ways, closely associating Mutabilitie with the Fall, yet not clearly blaming her for it. The result is a certain vagueness centering on **since which** in 6.5. Is Mutabilitie the cause of the Fall? or does the appearance of Change only mark the time of the Fall?

5. **wights,** 'creatures'.

6. **woxen,** 'grown'.

9. **sucked from our nurse.** The nurse is probably Nature, as in the 'Orphic Hymn'; cf. Curtius, *European Literature and the Latin Middle Ages*, tr. W. Trask (1953), p. 107.

7.3. **cast,** 'plan'.

5–7. This description of the 'region of the ayre' accords with Elizabethan astronomy, see *The Frame of Order* (1957), ed. J. Winney, p. 162.

8. **ne . . . contraire**, 'not oppose'.

8.9. Cumming, *SP* 28 (1931), 243–5, compares Mutabilitie's incursion to Phaeton's ride as told by Ovid in *Metamorphoses* 2, finding specific indebtedness in such details as the bright shining palace, the silver gates, and the assembly of deities to discuss the commotion caused by Phaeton's ride. Comes, 4.9, asserts that Fortune once rebelled against the Gods.

1. **clambe**, 'climbed', here both archaic and metaplastic.

4. **story**, 'structure', as in Spenser's *Muiopotomos, 327* and *Cymbeline* 2.2.27. Apparently Cynthia's palace walls were ornamented with depictions of the cosmic frame, a detail significant in view of Mutabilitie's attack on Order.

7. **Hight**, 'called'. **liefe or sory**, 'willing or not'.

8. This may refer to a 'floor' of the palace, yet according to Pontanus, *Urania* (1513), 2.23, 4.86, the air was divided into three layers which Du Bartas (*Works*), ed. Holmes, Lyons, Linker (1938), II, p. 237) calls 'estages'. **scand,** probably 'climbed', from *scandere*, rather than 'examined'. cf. *Shepheardes Calender* 'October', 88.

9. An unusual bit of word play with 'sit' ('having her seat of power') and 'stand' that sets the tone of the confrontation to follow.

9.2. The two steeds, suggesting the aspects of the moon, are found, according to Lotspeich, p. 54 in Boccaccio's *De Genealogia Deorum* 4.16 and in Comes 3.17. R. N. Ringler, in an unpublished Harvard dissertation (1961), p. 148, also traces them to Jean Lemaire de Belges' account of the marriage of Peleus and Thetis.

6. **intend**, 'call'.

10.7. **Eftsoones**, 'at once'. **tortious**, 'wrong', the legal overtone, from 'tort', is important.

9. **wained**, 'drawn'; see 8.7 for the image of the Moon's 'bright wagon'. Other editors suggest 'diminished' from the connection with 'waned', but this seems less likely.

11.3. **wend**, 'thought'. The connection with the story of Phaeton is clearest in the first half of this stanza.

5. That Mutabilitie here bemoans the Fall is both ironic and indicative of the complexity with which she is conceived.

6–8. The triple nature of the moon is suggested in these lines. Infernal powers were thought to receive the moon's light when it was not visible on earth. But perhaps 7–8 refer only to the notion of the moon as presiding over villainy; see *1 Henry IV* 1.2.

9. **condign**, 'worthy', a nonce-word in Spenser.

12.5. **cheare**, 'mood'.

6. In iconographic tradition Diana is represented with the crescent

9

(horn) above or near her forehead, as in the sculpture of Diana in the Capitoline Museum, Rome. Possibly here Spenser wants to allude also to the horned brow of Moses or the cornua of the mitre as symbolic of law-giving. But the horned moon is a descriptive commonplace as in *FQ* 4.6.49.3 and 7.7.50.8.

8. coast. The circle of the Moon is a boundary of heaven, dividing it from the sublunary realm. **pack**, used here as colloquially as it is today, cf. *FQ* 6.6.21.6.

13.1. nathemore, 'not in the least'.

2. preacing-on, 'pressing on'. **raught,** 'reached'.

4. Gold is not always a symbol of virtue. Actually a white rod is associated with benign powers in Spenser in *FQ* 2.9.27.7, 3.3.49.7, and 5.7.7.5.

14.4. vnpurvaide, 'lacking', a nonce-word.

6. The restoration of Chaos, from which all things originated (see *FQ* 3.6.36.8) was both a literary formula for great natural upset, as in *FQ* 4.9.23.9, and a real fear available for descriptions of upset psychological states as in Othello's famous 'and when I love thee not, Chaos is come again'. The conception of Chaos is derived from Hesiod, *Theog.* 123, where Night, significantly for this passage in the *Cantos*, is personified as Chaos' child (in Boccaccio's *Genealogy of the Gods* Night is the consort of Chaos), and from Ovid's account in *Met.* 1.5–20 of a primal mass of 'warring seeds'. The conception had great influence during the Renaissance and orthodox thinkers like Du Bartas identified Chaos with the formless void of *Genesis*. Empedocles' notion of the pacification of the warring elements through love had been Christianized, as in Spenser's *FQ* 4.9.35ff.: 'their Almightie Maker . . . bound them with inviolable bands; / Else would the waters overflow the lands.' It is these 'bands' whose rupture— and the subsequent end of divine control—is feared. Cf. Tillyard, *Elizabethan World Picture* (1944), pp. 13–15.

8. Following the Ptolemaic system, Spenser places Mercury nearest the moon. As messenger of the gods he was also the appropriate person to carry the alarm to Jove. As in medieval allegory, the planets are understood as mythological personages, see Tuve, *Allegorical Imagery* (1966), pp. 226–7, and Seznec, *The Survival of the Pagan Gods* (1952), pp. 39–40.

9. plaine, 'complain'.

15.8. Lotspeich, p. 113 and Starnes and Talbert, p. 75 show Spenser's debt to Comes 6.22 in identifying Typhon with Typhoeus, as one of the Giants most active in the rebellion against Jove. Comes interprets the myth as demonstrating *ambitionis furor*. Typhon, the largest monster ever born, was the issue of Earth and Tartarus; his assault caused terror among the gods (see 1.9), but finally Jove subdued him with thunderbolts and imprisoned him under Mount Aetna, from which he belches fire and smoke, appropriate to his name. Cf. Hesiod, *Theog.* 821ff. Spenser refers to Typhon-Typhoeus at several points in *FQ* and the *Visions of Bellay* as an archetype of the brutish rebel. See *FQ* 1.5.35.7, 6.6.11–12.

9. **fear'd**, 'frightened', see Abbott, pp. 202–3.

16.1. **sonne of Maia,** 'Mercury'.

4. **forslowe,** 'delay'.

6. Magical control of the sun and moon was a classical commonplace, as in Horace, *Epodes* 5.43 and Virgil, *Eclogues* 8.69. Spenser follows the tradition in *FQ* 3.3.12, where Merlin can make both sun and moon obey him 'by wordes'. Eclipses were thought to be especially subject to magic.

7. **attache,** 'sieze', or 'indict', originally a legal term and often used so, as in *2 Henry IV* 4.2.110.

9. **prest,** 'promptly'. The double standard of Jove's justice here is both proper and amusing.

17.1. **wingd-foot god,** 'Mercury', as in *Ruins of Time* 666, and in Ovid, *Met.* 4.756.

3. Spenser's refusal to describe this tussle for Cynthia's 'seat' demonstrates that he understands the slapstick possibilities of the situation. This is one instance where the 'drab' style, as C. S. Lewis would call it, serves a function other than economy.

4. **hardiness,** 'boldness'.

9. **discharge,** 'explain'.

18.2. The powers of the caduceus were earlier described in *FQ* 2.12.41, where it is also spoken of as permitting Mercury to tame 'infernall fiends' and rule the Furies. Lotspeich, p. 44, cites *Aeneid* 4.242ff. and Comes 5.5, where the caduceus is a symbol of concord.

6. Mutabilitie's tone and attitude are artfully conveyed in the word 'his', repeated in 8 and underlined there by 'him' and 'self' in 9. Her contempt reaches a climax in the word 'all' in 9, on which the metre dictates an especially heavy emphasis. The stanza is strongly conceived as dramatic speech.

8. **Sith,** 'since', becoming obsolete.

19.3–4. Like Milton's God, Jove sits in 'the pure Empyrean . . . high thron'd above all highth . . . . About him all the Sanctities of Heaven', *PL* 3.57–60. The Empyrean, the highest heaven, was a realm of pure fire. There is an obvious thematic reason for the infusion of 'Christian astronomy' here. Yet it should be apparent from the severe limitations on his power that Jove is not simply the symbol of a Christian God.

20. The influence of this and the following stanzas on Milton should be apparent in the tone and materials of the opening lines; cf. *PL* 2. 129, for example.

2. **since,** 'once'. **Earth's cursed seed,** 'the Titans'.

6, 7. The use of 'quite' here may conceal a touch of humour. Lotspeich, p. 55, traces the idea of new giants born of the blood of the old to *Met.* 1,151–62. Spenser may also have used Comes 6.20.

21.3. **Phoebe,** another name for Diana. This is the only point in the

Cantos at which this name is employed. Elsewhere, as in 'April', 65 of the *Calender*, and in 1.7.5.1, 2.2.44.1, Spenser employs the adjective 'fair', and it is possible that for Spenser Phoebe was associated with the feminine, vulnerable aspect of the moon, making it the epithet of choice for this context. He had of course employed the phrase earlier in the name of Belphoebe, a surrogate for Elizabeth in her aspect of a 'most vertuous and beautifull lady'. There are metrical considerations as well.

6. **advise,** 'consider'.

9. **Areed,** 'speak'. Despite the Miltonic overtones here one must recall that—Jove's appetites being what they were—many of his audience were in fact his sons.

22.2. **beck,** a gesture of summons. Jove's 'black eyebrow' is traditional, as in *Iliad* 1.528, and in Spenser's *Mother Hubberd's Tale* 1228. The same passage in Homer is echoed in 30 below. If Spenser were not elsewhere guilty of apparently arbitrary alliteration, one might suspect the alliteration in 2–3 of being deliberately comic.

3. **vow,** 'will'.

5. **degrees,** 'according to rank'.

9. **emprize,** 'undertaking'.

23.4. **re-allie,** 'get in order'.

5. **extasie,** 'bewilderment'. But the word may also carry connotations of the *extasis,* the going forth of soul from body, amusingly incongruous in this context.

7. **purest sky,** Jove's Empyrean seat was the region of the purest light. See F. R. Johnson, *Astronomical Thought in Renaissance England* (1937), p. 56.

9. **Good . . . end,** one of Spenser's frequent aphorisms, a variant of a common proverb, cf. M. P. Tilley, *A Dictionary of Proverbs in England* (1950), B259.

24.2. **close,** 'secret'.

5. **wist,** 'knew'. **chose,** a metaplastic form for the sake of the rhyme.

6. **aby,** 'remain', probably archaic.

9. **mote,** 'might', archaic. The construction, an example of chiasmus, demonstrates the workmanship Spenser often expended on the final line of a stanza. The attitude of Jove in this line and the one before it is in keeping with the comic treatment.

25.2. **All,** 'although'.

7. An amusing bit of administrative strategy.

8. **make,** 'want'.

9. The alexandrine easily absorbs an extra syllable before the medial break.

26.6. Lotspeich, p. 46, thinks Spenser follows Hesiod, *Theog.* 116 in making Chaos the parent of Earth. This is the third time Mutabilitie's ancestry is mentioned.

7. **father's,** Titan's.

27.2. Sawtelle, *Sources of Spenser's Classical Mythology* (1896), pp. 115–116, believes that Spenser depended on Comes 6.20 for this unusual account in which Saturn kills his children as a condition of reigning in Titan's place. In Hesiod, *Theog.* 453–67, and most classical mythographers, Saturn devoured his children to foil the prophecy that one would displace him. As Sawtelle observes, Comes' version best suits Spenser's aim.

4. **slight,** 'trickery'. Hesiod, *Theog.* 485ff. relates that the attendants of Jove's mother, Rhea or Cybele, beat shields and spears to cover the infant Jove's birth-cries. Cybele completed the deception of Saturn by offering Saturn a stone wrapped in swaddling clothes. This, Saturn proceeded to swallow, believing it the infant Jove. The story is told also in Ovid, *Fasti* 4.201–46.

5. **younger . . . elder,** 'Saturn . . . Titan'.

28.5. **in place,** 'on the spot', as in *FQ* 1.5.36.1.

6. **sort,** 'herd', 'group of', as in 'sort of bees' *FQ* 5.4.36.7. Spenser is consciously amusing here, and remembering the Homeric epithet of 'ox-eyed' or 'ox-faced' Hera.

9. **ghastly,** 'terrified'. **Bewray,** 'disclose'.

29. Jove's regal pause, his rhetorical question, and his refusal to deal directly with Mutabilitie's claim show Spenser's familiarity with the Establishment manner.

5. **hire,** 'punishment'. Procrustes, a robber of Attica, killed his victims by stretching or chopping them to fit a bed. Theseus punished him by his own Procrustean method. There is no classical precedent for his aspiration to heavenly rule or to his being punished by Jove. As Lotspeich suggests, p. 102, Spenser may be thinking of him vaguely as a rebellious giant and thus fit company for the others.

6. On **Typhon,** see note to 15.8 above. **Ixion** was bound to a fiery wheel for trying to seduce Hera. **Prometheus,** a Titan who stole fire from the gods for mankind, was bound to a rock. Each day a vulture ate his liver; each night it grew whole again. Lotspeich suggests that Spenser follows Comes 6.16 in this passage. He had employed Prometheus before as in *FQ* 2.10.70 and Ixion in *FQ* 1.5.35.1, both as types of rebellion.

8. **for to,** 'to'; see Abbott, pp. 102–3.

30.1. **off-scum,** 'refuse', refers specifically to Mutabilitie. **fry,** 'brood', here the line of the Titans.

2. **Dare.** Subject-verb disagreements in number are not uncommon in Elizabethan English, but here Spenser may intend to call attention to Mutabilitie's incursions as part of a collective act. Sugden, *The Grammar of Spenser's 'Faerie Queene'* (1936), p. 22, notes instances of the psychological plural in collectives.

4. Osgood, *Variorum* 7.280, notes the Latinate construction of this line as anticipating Milton.

6–8. The picture of Jove's wrath is traditional, cf. *Iliad* 1.528–30.

8. **eft,** 'then'. **quooke,** 'quaked', another metaplastic form.

9. **levin-brond,** 'lightning bolt'.

31. Spenser carefully differentiates the tones of successive stages in Jove's response: 29 begins magisterially, 30 with violence, 31 gently.

7. **flesh,** probably 'mortals'. But is Mutabilitie only 'flesh'? Upton cites Genesis 6.3 and Psalms 78.39 as similarly worded instances of God's forbearance.

8. Jove's concern for the continuity of humanity despite its sins is echoed in Diana's refusal to 'spill / The wood-god's breed, which must for ever live' in stanza 50. Both are related to the divine love that issues in the Chain of Being and the principle of Plenitude. See Tillyard, *Elizabethan World Picture,* chapter 4, and A. O. Lovejoy, *The Great Chain of Being* (1936), esp. chaps. IV, V. Divine concern with the continuity of species, rather than of individuals, is presented by Spenser in *FQ* 3.6.30–42. On the discussion relating to the concept of 'species' here, see C. S. Lewis, *Studies in Medieval and Renaissance Literature* (1966), p. 153.

9. **still,** 'always'.

32.1. **ween,** 'believe'.

3. **that,** 'what'.

5. **spight,** 'envy'. For Bellona as a Titan see note to 3.7 above.

33.3. **interesse,** 'legal right'.

5. R. N. Ringler, p. 218, notes that in his *View of the Present State of Ireland,* Spenser accepts the common view that conquest confers the right of sovereignty.

6. Golding, in the 'Epistle' to his translation of Ovid, explains that Christians will interpret 'Fate' in pagan writers as 'the order which is set . . . / By Gods eternall will and word. . . .' The interpretation stems from Boccaccio 1.5.8–9. The import is clear, though the syntax is murky, and the word order tortured. Jove reserves not only the rule over heaven, but the right to judge who is worthy to share its bliss. On the vagaries of Elizabethan prepositions, see Abbott, pp. 93ff. 'To whom' probably has the force of 'for which'.

34.3. C. S. Lewis, *Studies,* p. 152, observes that 'there is no need to identify . . . Titan at all rigorously with Satan', as Ellrodt does in *Neoplatonism in the Poetry of Spenser* (1960). 'It is enough that there should be an analogy; Titan is to Jove as Satan to God.'

4. **faine,** 'wish'.

7. **Saturne's sonne.** This substitution of epithet for name is intended to be insulting, as was Jove's 'foolish gerle' in 1.

35.1. **equall,** 'impartial'.

2. **dewfull,** a coinage.

4–6. The identity of the 'highest him' is somewhat unclear; the phrase surely suggests the Christian deity, as does 'Father of gods and men', but it is difficult to say whether 'god of Nature' is an appositive or objective genitive, and Dame Nature, in VII.5 below, is bisexual or of doubtful sex, as in the tradition, cf. Introd., 'Nature'. However, it is clear that Mutabilitie appeals beyond Jove to Nature, and that Spenser intends the Christian overtones. M. Hughes, *PMLA* 41 (1926), 555, suggests an echo of the appeal to natural law in sixteenth-century jurisprudence. On the use of pronouns with attributive adjectives as nouns, see Sugden, p. 30, and Abbott, p. 224.

9. **Dan Phoebus Scribe.** Lotspeich, p. 37, thinks this unprecedented use of Apollo as secretary is an extension of his office as singer. The line is a piece of irony; the 'gods' are 'cut down to size' by Mutabilitie's appeal.

36.3. The trial before Nature was probably suggested to Spenser by Chaucer's *Parlement of Foulys*, see Introd., 'Literary Antecendents'.

6-8. **Arlo Hill** is the highest head or peak in a range—called by Spenser Mole—running east from near Buttevant in County Cork to Galtymore (Arlo Hill itself) in County Limerick. Galtymore, slightly over 3,000 feet high, is close to the site of Spenser's home, Kilcolman Castle, and was probably named Arlo by Spenser because it overlooks the Vale of Aherlow in County Tipperary. The Aherlow River joins the Suir, **Shure,** mentioned in 54.9 below. The whole Arlo area was rich in Irish folklore. Cf. P. W. Joyce, *Frazer's Magazine*, n.s. 17 (1878), 325-6, 330; R. M. Smith, *PMLA* 50 (1935), 1049.

8-9. Spenser had written of 'father Mole' in *Colin Clout's Come Home Again* 57, 104, 110, to whose pastoral conventions 8 and 9 refer. The reference is an interesting mixture of *amour propre* and convention which effects an easy transition to first person commentary in the next stanza.

37.1. **And were it not . . . I would.** 'If it is not inappropriate . . . I should like to.' **file,** 'catalogue', a nonce-word in Spenser, but used several times in Shakespeare. Spenser is still thinking of the 'records permanent' of 2.5 above.

4. **stounds,** 'conflicts', an archaism, apparently revived by several early Tudor poets; cf. Rubel, *Poetic Diction in the English Renaissance* (1941), pp. 21, 85.

7. **holy island.** The antiquity of Irish Christianity and letters was generally acknowledged in England. Spenser alludes to it several times in his *View of Ireland* and refers, with a bitter pun, to that *sacra insula,* on p. 145 of the *Variorum* edition.

9. Has Clio, the muse of history, been presiding over the earlier stanzas, and is she now asked to aid Calliope, who will tell the Faunus story? Or has Calliope, the epic muse, been presiding all along, and is she now to borrow Clio's pen? The point is much debated, notably by Padelford, *SP* 27 (1930), 111-24; Bennett, *JEGP* 31 (1932); Starnes, *Univ. of Texas Studies* (1942), 31-58. A clear resolution is prevented by Spenser's ambiguity here, in the opening of canto VII, and in the Proem to *FQ* 1. Further, the conflicting traditions regarding the functions of the Muses (see Curtius, pp. 229-230, 234), do not permit us to decide which muse is 'chiefe of nyne'

in the Proem or the 'greater muse' in canto VII, though Lotspeich, p. 84, argues for Clio. If Spenser is a 'poet historicall', and concerned with the 'files' of Faery, he is also consciously writing epic. And if the Faunus digression is pastoral (thus according to some sources, subject to Calliope), it is also 'historical' in telling a 'true story' of Ireland, and in its current political implications. My own guess, it can be no more than that, is that Clio here lends her pen to Calliope, and resumes her function as presiding muse when the Faunus story is over.

38.1–3. From the sixth to the ninth centuries Irish culture was pre-eminent in the north of Europe, as Spenser was aware in the *View of Ireland*. **wealths.** Hughes (1715) conjectures that this is an error for 'wealth', possibly, according to the *Variorum* editor, a compositor's misreading of *-es* for *-e* and a consequent failure to set the *-e*.

7 Cynthia. A name for Diana, the virgin huntress of classical myth, here a complimentary allusion to Elizabeth.

9. then, 'than'. The two are frequently interchanged in Elizabethan English. **on ground,** 'on earth', an accurate description of Irish rivers and climate.

39.2–6. The syntax seems to wander here because of misleading parallelism resulting from Spenser's anaphora in the repetition of on. The passage from **Either** to **belowe** should be taken as parenthetical, and **or . . . or** in 5 read as 'Either . . . or' (cf. Abbott, p. 92), and as applying specifically to **flowe.**

40.2. Molanna is Spenser's name for the Behanagh River, about sixteen miles east of Kilcolman. The name suggests a telescoping of Mole and Behanagh, cf. R. B. Gottfried, *SP* 34 (1937), 108.

3–6. Mulla is Spenser's name for the Awbeg River, another stream near Kilcolman, probably derived from Kilnemullah, an ancient place-name of the area. Mulla's affair with the Bregog was told **dearely,** or 'lovingly', in *Colin Clout's Come Home Again* 104–55.

7. shole, 'shallow', here a pun. The Behanagh is, in fact, shallower than the Awbeg. Spenser's Irish topography is accurate throughout; see Joyce, *loc. cit.*, 328–9 on the details of this and the following stanzas.

41.2. The oaks were probably an accurate descriptive detail, see A. C. Judson, *Spenser in Southern Ireland* (1933), pp. 37–43, yet the oak is also a symbol of Diana.

4. pompous, 'splendid' or 'ceremonious'.

5. bowre . . . strowes, 'room, which many flowers strew'; here used with a singular rather than plural ending. There is no distortion for rhyme's sake; Shakespeare rhymes 'strew' with 'go' in *Cymbeline* 4.2.287.

42. In the Faunus episode, Spenser re-works three stories from Ovid's *Metamorphoses*: the stories of Actaeon and Diana, Diana's punishment of Calisto, and the love of Alpheus for Aretheusa. Spenser may also owe something to Comes' retelling of the myths (6.24) and to Irish folktale, cf. R. M. Smith, *loc. cit.*, 1047–56. See Introd., 'Faunus and Diana', where the political and ethical implications of the episode are also treated.

7. Faunus, like Pan, a god of the forest. Here, as in classical and Renaissance art generally, he is represented as a type of Lechery. He appears earlier chasing a nymph in *FQ* 2.2.7–9. Lotspeich, p. 60, observes parallels to his character in Horace, *Odes* 3.18.1.

43.1. **compasse**, 'achieve'.

2. **discouer**, 'disclose'.

4. **assaide**, 'tried'.

5. The **Queene-apple** is identified variously as the 'quince', from '*mala Cydonia*' (ME 'guyne', 'coin', see note in *Variorum*, *Calender* 'June', 43); the 'Quarrenden apple', see *Poetical Works of William Basse*, ed. Bond (1893), p. 238; and by *OED.* as the 'rennet'. The gift of fruit is traditional in pastoral from Theocritus on as in *Calender*, 'June', 43. The apple could be symbolic of 'obstinacion', as in de Deguileville's *Pèlerinage de la Vie Humaine*, cf. Tuve, *Allegorical Imagery* (1966), pp. 168–9; the cherry of the soul's reward for merit and piety, cf. Friedmann, *The Symbolic Goldfinch* (1946), p. 95. The passage is discussed in Introd., 'Faunus and Diana'.

44.2. **quit**, 'repay'.

4. The **Fanchin** is Spenser's name for the Fansheon River, which is joined by the Behanagh (Molanna) near the bridge of Kilbeheny.

8. **moe**, a Chaucerian variant for 'more', carried over into early Tudor verse.

45.3. **That**, 'what'. **one**, Actaeon, the luckless voyeur of Ovid's tale. This is an instance of Spenser's habit of using a classical myth as both pattern and simile for his own invention, cf. Lotspeich, p. 9.

4. **to so foole-hardy**, 'to one so foolhardy'.

5. **hew**, the usual gloss is 'appearance', and this is the most common meaning of the word in Spenser. In Ovid's version, Actaeon is killed, not in hunter's garb, but after he had been changed to a stag in *Metamorphoses* 3.155ff. Yet **hew** can also mean 'destruction', as in *FQ* 6.8.49.6, though this is a unique instance in Spenser. **Hew** can also mean (as in 'hue and cry') the shout that once according to law obliged all within hearing to join in pursuit of a felon. The usual gloss is preferable, though possibly the association with 'hue and cry' is intended.

6. **Tho**, 'then', a common variant.

9. This should recall Jove's susceptibility to Mutabilitie's charms and further dispel notions of his supposed identity with God.

46.3. **some-what**, 'something'. One is tempted to recall here Tucker Brooke's remark that Spenser was one of the few English poets who wrote about sex 'like a gentleman'.

8. **conceit**, 'thought'. **areed**, 'reveal'. The line is awkward metrically.

9. **meed**, 'gain'.

47.5. **darred**, 'dazed'. Larks were trapped after being dazzled by pieces of scarlet cloth or by a 'dare', a circular board with bits of glass imbedded in it, or simply by a mirror. Sometimes the lark was so fascinated by a manoeuvring hawk as not to see the net; cf. Shakespeare, *Henry VIII* 3.2.283. The simile is especially apt. The sound-play: **darred-daring, larke-look,** is typical of Spenser at his technical best.

8. **nought,** 'useless'; cf. *FQ* 2.9.32.

48.1. **huswife,** 'housewife'. Upton finds a similarity between this ludicrous simile and the passage in which Ariosto compares the necromancer Atalanta to a cat and his intended victim, Bradamante, to a mouse. The simile is, at any rate, assurance that Faunus' fate, and the outcome of the episode, will not be tragic, and so is well placed.

3. **vnware,** 'unexpectedly'.

6. **gin,** 'contrivance'.

7. **traine,** 'lure'.

49.2. **baile,** 'power'.

5. **haile,** 'pull'; plucking the beard was a culminating insult, as in *Hamlet* 2.2.600.

6. Spenser here shows Faunus some of the amused indulgence he shows Mutabilitie.

9. **mome,** 'blockhead'.

50.3. **same would spill,** 'the gelding would destroy'; cf. note to 31.8 above.

5. **driue,** Sugden, p. 94, thinks the omission of *-en* here may be a 'Chaucerism'.

51.4. **straighter sort,** 'more closely'.

8. **bewraid,** 'revealed'.

9. The omission of 'they' before **laid** is here justified by the illusion of rapid action. Sugden, p. 11, thinks the construction archaic.

52.5. **aghast,** 'terrified'.

7. **brast,** 'burst', an instance of metathesis, here for the sake of rhyme. The propriety of such alterations is discussed in Introd., 'Diction'.

8–9. The reminiscence of the refrain of Spenser's *Epithalamion* is ironic here.

53.4. **whelm'd,** 'overwhelmed'; the dreadful punishment is ironically negated by what Gottfried, *loc. cit.*, 108 calls an 'etiological myth'. The later part of the course of the Behanagh is actually clogged by stones; cf. *Colin Clout's Come Home Again* 148ff. for a similar tale about the Bregog. **for her paine,** 'for Molanna's efforts'.

8. **bed,** a pun on 'river bed'. The tale of Alphaeus and Arethusa, on which Spenser bases the Molanna-Fanchin story, was allegorized in Comes 6.25 as the desire of imperfection to unite with virtue. One can see the same 'evolutionary' striving in the pageant of the months. Cf. Introd., 'Iconography'.

54.1. **Nath'lesse,** 'nevertheless'.

8. **champian,** 'countryside'; probably a compositor's error for 'champain'. **rid,** 'seen', p.p. of 'read'.

9. **Shure.** See note to 36.6–8 above. For the reference of this stanza and the next to Elizabeth's troubles with Ireland, see Introd., 'Faunus and Diana'.

55.1. **way,** 'consider'.

3. **haplesse,** 'Bearing misfortune'.

4. **space,** 'Roam'.

6. **chase,** 'Hunting ground'.

CANTO VII

Proem. 1. **Pealing,** aphaeresis for 'appealing'. **Bar,** 'court'. Fowler, *Spenser and the Courts of Love* (1921), p. 68, asserts Spenser's debt to the medieval Court of Love tradition for some details in this canto, but the primary antecedent for the Nature's court material seems to be Chaucer's *Parlement*.

2. **Alteration,** another name for Mutabilitie.

3. **Large,** 'extensive'.

4. **Doome,** 'decision'. **areads,** 'proclaims'.

1.1. **greater,** see note on 37.9 above.

3–4. The affectation (or expression) of modesty was conventional in the exordium of elevated verse, see Curtius, *op. cit.*, pp. 83ff., and in classical legal procedure.

6. **(Thy soueraine sire).** Jove was father of Apollo, hence grand-sire of the Muses. **his,** an old genitive form common until the early seventeenth century. Abbott, p. 144, thinks it the result of a scribal confusion of his with 's.

7. **bigger,** 'louder', possibly a Virgilian echo; cf. Spenser's *Virgil's Gnat* 11, and Virgil, *Eclogues* 4.1.

2.2. **weaker,** 'too weak', a Latinate construction; cf. Sugden, p. 13n.

3. **turne,** 'verses of praise', from a rendering of the Gr. *strophe*, as in the sub-heads of Ben Jonson's 'To the Immortal Memory and Friendship of . . . Sir Lucius Cary, and Sir H. Morison'. **feeble.** In the Newberry copy, 'sable'; probably a compositor's misreading of the ms. hand. The suggestion that the line requires no emendation, sable being 'black', as if in reference to an exhausted fire, is over-ingenious, and neglects the pejorative overtones of the phrase 'sable breast'.

6–9. The passage recalls the invocation of Urania in Spenser's *Tears of the Muses* 499–522, and so Urania ('the heavenly one') has been suggested as the muse invoked here. This only complicates an already insoluble problem.

3.4. **other world,** 'Earth'.

6. **powers.** Probably refers also to the intermediate hierarchy of fallen angels on the Dionysian system. See Ephesians 6.12, Colossians 2.15, and note to canto VI.3.4 above. The absence of infernal powers is inevitable: natural order depends on their incarceration; evil, on the Boethian (and Augustinian) view Spenser shared, was not of nature; it was un-natural, 'non-being'. Hence infernal powers could hardly be among Nature's train.

8. **they,** both the divine and the heavenly creatures.

9. **Pluto and Proserpina,** the king and queen of Hell, are appropriately present as members of 'the race of gods', and because of Proserpina's rôle in fertility and the regulation of the seasons. She was the daughter of Jove and Ceres, goddess of agriculture. Proserpina was kidnapped by Pluto, and the resulting squabble was patched up after an agreement that Proserpina spend three (winter) months with Pluto, the rest on earth with Ceres. Kahin, *ELH* 8 (1941), notes the appearance of the pair at a similar assembly, and R. N. Ringler, p. 289–90, in urging Jean Lemaire de Belges, *Illustrations d Gaule et Singularitez de Troye* as a possible source for stanzas 1–12^e notes that Pluto and Proserpina are present at the nuptials of Peleus, and Thetis, see stanza 12 below. However, in Claudian, *De Raptu Proserpina*, Nature is portrayed as herself wedding Proserpine to Pluto. Apparently no specific 'source' need be invoked.

4. There are many literary parallels to this assembly of creation, fecundity being a commonplace in the depiction of Dame Nature. Spenser seems closest, however, to the assembly in Chaucer's *Parlement* 306–8, 313–15.

6. Order appears as the marshal of Mercilla's palace in *FQ* 5.9.23. His presence here already suggests that Mutabilitie's case (cf. 5.2–3 above) is lost, and the personification of Order—in the *Parlement* 320 Nature herself arranges her creatures—suggests the emphasis Spenser wants put on that presence, as do the three lines given his activity.

5. For the tradition of Dame Nature, see Introd., 'Nature'.

5. **physnomy,** 'countenance'.

6–8. The uncertain sex of Nature was possible suggested by Plutarch's statue of Isis in *De Iside et Osiride* 9, or by Spenser's own description of the veiled hermaphrodite Venus in *FQ* 4.10.41, another embodiment of fecundity. C. S. Lewis, *Studies*, p. 153, cites as 'affinities' with the bisexuality and veil of Nature, Cusanus, *Doct. Ignorantia* 25 and Macrobius' commentary on the *Dream of Scipio* 1.2.17. Vagueness in the description of Nature is a common instance of the 'inexpressibility' topos, see Curtius, pp. 159–62. The paradoxes regarding Nature in stanza 13 below fostered the strategy.

7. **descry,** 'perceive'; cf. *Roman de la Rose* 16248.

8. **wimpled,** 'lay in folds'.

9. On **was** for 'were', see Sugden, p. 24, whose examples involve only the words 'face', 'soul', and 'hands'—suggesting a restricted use of this construction.

6.2. vncouth hue, 'strange appearance'.

3. agrized, 'horrified'.

4. Some editors suggest the image comes directly from Alain of Lille's *De Planctu Naturae,* one of Chaucer's sources for the *Parlement.* In Prose 1, Nature's zodiacal diadem has a lion represented in the first stone. Yet it is unlikely Spenser had read Alain. The lion is commonly a sign of power, at times of Christ, cf. Tuve, *Allegorical Imagery,* pp. 123–354.

8. pass, 'surpass'. The image may have been suggested by Chaucer's *Parlement* 299–301.

9. Cf. 2 Corinthians 3.18. There are several such minor reverberations of a suggested association of Nature with the Christian God. For the tradition drawn on here see Taylor, *Milton's Use of Du Bartas* (1934), p. 42.

7.2. Sat, 'exercised judicial authority'.

3. sheene, 'beautiful'.

5–9. Spenser can find no comparison for Nature's garment nor for the cloth that Peter, James, and John saw Christ wearing when they witnessed His transfiguration. See Matthew 17.1–8; Mark 9.2–3. Actually the garments *are* compared, and the point of Nature's association with renewal (as contrasted with mutability) and divinity is made. Spenser continues his posture of humility and suggests, in his own dazzlement at Nature, his association with the attitude of the saints.

8.1. equall, 'symmetrical'.

3. as, in some 1609 copies 'ar', obviously a printing error. **idle,** 'vain'.

4. states, 'dignity'.

5–7. In the Court of Love environment the natural arbor was not uncommon, cf. *Parlement* 30–5 and E. B. Fowler, pp. 25–6. The unusual usage here suggests the Latin *sua sponte*.

9.3. Dan Geffrey, 'Master Geoffrey Chaucer'. **spright,** 'noble spirit'.

5. mel, 'meddle', not really a rare or archaic word, despite E. K.'s glossing of it for Spenser's *Calender* 'July', 208.

6–9. Alane. Alain of Lille (1128?–1202) the poet and Platonizing theologian, whose *De Planctu Naturae* Chaucer cites in *Parlement* 316–18 for those who wish to see Nature described. Spenser is having fun here, esp. in 9. As Upton suggests, it is doubtful if Spenser ever read him. The work circulated only in manuscript in Spenser's time, and its title is incorrectly given; it would be *Kynde,* as it is in Chaucer, not *Kindes* as here.

10. The stanza is a set piece in the tradition of the pleasance (*locus amoenus*), for which see Curtius, pp. 195–200, and Fowler, pp. 19–20. The analogous passage in Chaucer's *Parlement* is 183–6.

2. dight, 'decked'. **voluntary.** The homage of spontaneous flowering appears in Homer, *Iliad* 14.347 and Hesiod, *Theog.* 194.

4. **mores,** 'plants'.

8–9. As in 8.3–4 above, Spenser emphasizes here the superiority of Nature over Art, of celestial over temporal pomp. Henry VIII had been an almost manaical collector of tapestries, and they were throughout Spenser's time a favourite adornment of rooms of state and grand private apartments. See, for example, the 'tapestry of silk and silver' Shakespeare places in Imogen's bedchamber, *Cymbeline* 2.4.68. Spenser seems to have been impressed by such hangings, many of which had allegorical themes, as is shown by the extensive description of the tapestry in Busyrane's castle in *FQ* 3.11.28–46, and by his references to tapestry elsewhere; cf. F. Hard, *Variorum* 3, Appendix VIII. The stanza itself with its delight in floral detail is suggestive of a common tapestry motif. **Painted,** unless taken in the general sense of 'depicted', cannot refer to the tapestries themselves, for 'painted' or 'steyned' cloths, found primarily in quite modest Elizabethan homes, were only cheap imitations of tapestry, like the 'waterworks' the Hostess had to pawn to give money to Falstaff in *2 Henry IV* 2.1.162. However, tapestries were not the only mode of wall decoration, and it is possible that **with** in 9 means 'together with' and that **painted imagery** refers either to easel paintings or wall decorations, such as those described in *FQ* 3.11.51, where Spenser clearly shows his knowledge of what a tapestry is.

9. **adorne.** Collective nouns are sometimes construed as plural, see Sugden, p. 162.

11.5. **tire,** 'adorn his head'. **oaken** because of the oak grove near the river.

6–7. Contrast this with the depiction of Faunus; this is hardly an instance of the 'Puritanism' sometimes wrongly attributed to Spenser in the *Cantos*.

8. Church recalls that Mole is gray in *Colin Clout's Come Home Again* 104.

9. **well beseene,** 'well treated', as in *FQ* 5.10.17, with connotations of the adjectival use of the phrase as 'good looking' in *FQ* 1.12.8.

12. Jove decided to marry off the sea-nymph, Thetis, to Peleus, after learning that any son of hers would be more powerful than his father. Thetis, however, objected to marrying a mortal, and Peleus, on advice, seized her as she lay asleep in a cave. A struggle ensued during which Thetis assumed various shapes, but finally Peleus subdued her. Classical sources place the wedding on Mount Pelion rather than Haemus Hill. Spenser knew the story in Ovid, *Met.* 11, and was possibly led to place the wedding on Haemus by the reference to 'Haemonia' in 229, as Upton suggests. In any case, the Peleus-Thetis story is appropriate to the *Cantos* because of its theme of the union of mortal and immortal after metamorphosis and guided human effort.

5. **pointed,** 'appointed'. **Peleus,** 'Pelene' in the Newberry copy.

7. R. N. Ringler, p. 336, notes that Claudian, *Epithalamium de Nuptiis Honori Augusti*, pref. 17–22 has Apollo singing the 'spousall hymne', but Upton thinks the line an allusion to Catullus' *Epithalamium*.

13.1. Nature, as mother of Earth, is grandmother of all creatures.

2. **eld,** 'old age'. A commonplace; for the tradition of the 'old woman and girl' topos, see Curtius, pp. 101–5, which precedes a study of the Goddess Natura.

2. The idea of youth in age is the first of a series of 'joined contraries', the figure synoeciosis. The others in the series are 'moouing, yet vnmoued', and 'Vnseene of any, yet of all beheld'.

3. The God of Nature is similarly addressed in Boethius, *Consolation of Philosophy,* as Upton pointed out, and suggests also the Aristotelian view of the deity as the 'unmoved mover' of all things, an idea absorbed into Christian thought. This presentation of Nature foretells her verdict against Mutabilitie.

4. The paradox, again, is associated with descriptions of God as in Exodus 24.15, and was a commonplace in Renaissance thought, see G. D. Taylor, p. 42, and Milton's *PL* 3.375, 2.264.

7–8. **feld,** 'prostrated'. Sudgen, p. 157, suggests that Spenser may be recalling here the confusion of ME forms of 'fall' and 'fell'. Mutabilitie's prostration before Nature shows that this is hardly a 'modern' rebellion such as the Platonic theology of the Renaissance might have mounted. Cf. C. S. Lewis, *Studies,* p. 152.

9. **amplifie,** 'to make impressive', see Tuve, *Elizabethan and Metaphysical Imagery* (1947), pp. 89–90, on the meaning of the word in Renaissance rhetoric. It carries also the suggestion of loudness.

14. R. N. Ringler, pp. 345–8, suggests that Mutabilitie's speech is patterned on Cicero's study of judicial oratory in *De Inventione*. The form of the speech is treated extensively in Rix, Appendix C.

2. See note to canto VII.1.1. above. R. N. Ringler remarks on the irony of a modest Mutabilitie.

4. **indifferently,** 'impartially'.

7. One does not know how much stock to put in the parentheses here. If the line is parenthetical and relates to the injuries **creatures doe to other,** then the meaning of **vnequally** as 'unfairly' is clear. But the line may be parallel to **Damning,** in which case **vnequally** would mean 'as their superior'. The former is probably the case, though it is tempting to see **vnequally ... equall** as a continuation of the paradoxes in stanza 13.

9. The idea of Nature as joining together all creatures was proverbial, as in *Parlement* 381, and in Ulysses' 'touch of Nature' that 'makes the whole world kin'. A collection of references may be found in Paré, *Les Idées et les lettres au XIIIe Siècle: le Roman de la Rose* (1947), pp. 73ff.

15.2. **faine,** 'pretend': 'And those who pretend to be his fellow god'.

3. **challenge,** 'claim'.

5. **in fee,** 'as an hereditary estate'; in feudal law, a fief.

6–9. A clever bit of false argument; since Nature controls heaven and earth, they are therefore alike, and what's good enough for Nature is good enough for Mutabilitie. She has earth, why not Heaven also?

16.2. **that,** 'what'.

5. **principality,** 'office of rule', but see also note to Canto VI.3.4. 7–8. Osgood, in *Variorum* 7.299, suggests the possibility of a reference to Mary Stuart's claim to the throne on the basis of descent from her great-grandfather Henry VII. K. Woodworth, *PMLA* 59 (1944), thinks Mutabilitie is Arabella Stuart, and relates the attempts to promote her claim to the throne.

17.1. **mauger,** 'despite'.

2. **most regiment,** 'greatest power'. 'Most' is frequently used in Elizabethan English as the superlative of 'great', cf. *Hamlet* 1.5.180.

3. Mutabilitie asks the court's leave here to do the expected, that is, to divide her matter for logical exposition.

4. **inholders,** 'occupants'. **conuent,** 'assemble'. A unique instance in Spenser, but apparently current; a similar form occurs once in Shakespeare, *Twelfth Night* 5.1.391.

5. **incontinent,** 'at once'.

7. **only,** 'alone'.

18. The presentation which follows, according to Cumming, *SP* 28 (1931), suggests Ovid, *Met.* 15.239–49 and elsewhere. Greenlaw, *SP* 17 (1920), argues for Lucretius, *De Rerum Naturae* 5.275–305, and elsewhere on the grounds of a similarity in the order of materials. See Introd., 'Literary Antecedents'.

4. The argument and phrasing here are similar to those of the extremist Giant in *FQ* 5.2.37 and 40, but suggest also the fertility cycle of The Garden of Adonis, *FQ* 3.6.36ff. Spenser's readers, catching both echoes, would have noted that Mutabilitie understands something, but not all, of the process of nature.

5. **crime,** 'corruption', with perhaps overtones of 'judgment', from Lat *crimen*.

7. **prime,** 'spring'.

8–9. See Ovid, *Met.* 15.177ff., 361–78; Lucretius, *De Re. Nat.* 1.56ff. 248, 543–50. Yet the alteration and continuity of Nature were surely commonplaces both of belief and observation.

19.2. **massacred.** The force of the word is perhaps an echo of Pythagoras' vehement vegetarianism in Ovid, *Met.* 15.94ff.

20. Details in this stanza, as in those above, may be found in Ovid, *Met.* 15.308 or Lucretius, *De Re. Nat.* 5.261, yet all are Renaissance commonplaces associated with Mutabilitie and occur frequently, as in Shakespeare's sonnet 64 or Montaigne's essay on cannibals, to name two instances at random.

2. **those same on high,** the clouds, see 1.8, cf. Genesis 1.7. This is formal speech and one must imagine the appropriate gestures in this line.

4. **still,** 'continually'.

5. **Ne any lake,** 'nor is there any'. This kind of ellipsis is quite common; see Abbott, pp. 290–1.

9. **streight,** 'suddenly'.

21.4. **randon,** 'random'. The spelling follows the old French origin. Sugden, p. 21 notes that Spenser uses the uninflected form 'fish' here but the inflected 'fishes' in 43 below.

7. **grange,** 'dwelling'.

22.2. **middle meane,** the medium for the functioning of all the senses.

3. Perhaps here Spenser recalls Lucretius' idea in *De Re. Nat.* (5.273–8 that men would dissolve if the air did not deposit on them (as) on all objects) the miniscule particles they continually shed. But the line may also extend the meaning of the previous line, by referring to air as the medium of the 'influence' of planets on man.

4. **his thin spirit,** 'its thin essence'. Of the four elements air, next to fire, was the least 'clogged with weight'. In Ovid, *Met.* 15.248ff. air is pictured as 'thickening' into water. The idea is a commonplace of Renaissance science.

6. **tickle,** 'unstable'.

9. The common notion of the winds as seriously affecting human life and health is given fullest expression by Milton in *PL* 10.692ff., where the 'Outrage from lifeless things' is related to the Fall.

23. R. N. Ringler, p. 394, points out that the stanza has resemblances to Du Bartas 1.2.389ff.

2. **her creatures.** The creatures of the air, yet the stanza applies equally to man.

7. For the origin of idea of 'penance' in connection with weather see note to 22.9.

9. Spenser has in mind here meteors, comets, and the aurora. Most such phenomena were thought to foretell disastrous alterations in human affairs.

24.1–2. The permanence of fire is crucial evidence for the medieval cast of Spenser's astronomy and his thought as a whole; see C. S. Lewis, *Studies,* p. 152, and compare with Donne's famous line 206 in 'The First Anniversary'. The 'putting out' of the element of fire in Donne's day was accomplished by the 'new' science, which demonstrated the falsity of the ancient notion that the earth was surrounded by a region of air which, in turn, enclosed both water and earth. This sublunary region of fire had to be postulated because of the transcience of such phenomena as meteors and the aurora, which could not possibly have come from the immutable regions of empyrean fire. This essentially Aristotelian scheme was broken by the appearance of a super-nova in Cassiopeia in 1572. Investigation revealed that this star was, in fact, beyond the 'circle' of the moon. The comet of 1577 gave further proof of the falsity of the old cosmology; see F. R. Johnson, *Astronomical Thought in Renaissance England* (1937), pp. 154–5. Spenser seems unaware of the implications of these events, or of the events themselves; at least Mutabilitie makes no attempt to deny the old natural framework by playing what C. S. Lewis calls 'her ace of trumps', the Nova of 1572. The idea of the immortality of fire goes back to its ancient association with the procreative principle and appears in various forms in myth and the Bible, see R. B. Onians, *Origins of European Thought* (1954), pp. 155ff., 489ff. In this stanza Mutabilitie seems not to make the distinction she makes in 26.4–5 between ethereal and 'domestic' or **usuall** fire. To do so would have been to weaken her argument.

3. **his,** 'its'. Abbott, p. 151, thinks his the commonly used genitive of 'it' as well as of 'he'. On the syntax of **which . . . parts,** see Sugden, p. 65.

8–9. If we are correct in dating the *Cantos,* the burning of Spenser's estate would help to explain the force of these lines.

25. **fower,** the four elements. The simplest introduction to the doctrine of the four elements, of which God made the world and man, is Tillyard, pp. 55ff.

3. The idea of the transformation of the elements is treated by Ovid in *Met.* 15.244–51, and by Lucretius in *De Re. Nat.* 1.738ff.

4. **slights,** 'devices'.

6. **sheere,** 'bright, clear'.

9. The agreement-in-conflict of the elements was a medieval commonplace, cf. Tuve, *SP* 30 (1933), 137.

26.4–5. See note to 24.1–2 above. This common distinction between Vesta and Vulcan follows classical and Renaissance mythography as in Comes 2.6 and 8.19, this, Earthly fire, used for domestic and manufacturing purposes.

6–7. Ops, Juno, and Neptune are also presented conventionally here, as in Boccaccio 3.2 and Comes 2.4.

8. This reference tenuously connects the main tale with the Faunus digression and 'explains' the apparent anti-climax in descending from major gods to quite minor figures.

9. **be,** 'are'. See Abbott, p. 212, for the indicative use of 'be'.

27.1. **approuen,** 'prove'. **En** was among the inflections being discarded during the Elizabethan period. Opinion differs on whether its use is to be considered conscious archaism, cf. Sugden, p. 110, McElderry, *PMLA* 47 (1932), 156.

3. **in being hold.** The general sense is clear, but one cannot be precise. 'Maintain' is perhaps an adequate gloss.

5. **the which.** This construction is common after previous use of the pronoun, see Abbott, p. 185. **in generall,** 'collectively'.

8–9. Nature's procedure is both leisurely and according to protocol, and Mutabilitie here is less rebel than lawyer.

28. In this stanza and in 44 Spenser employs only two rhymes. Both stanzas mark divisions in the material, and it is possible Spenser

intended the rhyme restriction to emphasize these divisions. Numerous classical 'sources' for the pageants have been proposed, among them *Met.* 2.25ff. and *De Re. Nat.* 5.737ff. But the materials were the property of medieval art and craft, see Ruskin, *Stones of Venice* 2.7.52, and Tuve, *Seasons and Months* (1933). Spenser would have come on them in innumerable forms. The transcendental implications of the pageant, also treated in the Introd., 'Iconography', are fully discussed by Hawkins in 'Mutabilitie and the Cycle of the Months' in *Form and Convention in the Poetry of Spenser*, ed. W. Nelson (1961).

7. **stoures,** 'conflicts', a favourite archaism with Spenser.

8. **morion.** A helmet without face-guard.

9. **that,** 'so'. Spring was the season of both amorous and military adventure.

29.5. **chauffed,** 'heated'.

8. **libbard,** 'leopard'. McElderry thinks this indicates the current pronunciation, rather than an archaism.

30.9. **yold,** 'yielded'. Spenser uses this oddity twice in *FQ* 3.11.17.4; it is archaic and was glossed by Speght in his 1598 edition of Chaucer, as was stoures above.

31.1. **frize,** a coarse woollen. This is probably an intentional pun.

4. **bill,** 'nose'.

5. **limbeck,** 'alembic', a vessel used in distilling. Possibly this line and 29.5 are recollections of Chaucer's Canon's Yeoman.

9. **loosed,** 'weak'. **weld,** 'control'.

32.1. **softly,** 'slowly', as befits seasons of the year. The swifter months ride.

3. Until the adoption of the Gregorian calendar by Great Britain in the mid-eighteenth century, the legal year began on March 25, Lady Day. In popular usage however the year began in January, as it does in Spenser's *Calender*. Spenser's choice of the older order here is appropriate to the religious theme and the motif of renewal in the *Cantos*.

4. March is the month of Mars, hence armed. As do the other months, March rides on its zodiacal sign, the ram Aries. Jove assumed the form to seduce Helle, after whom the Hellespont was supposedly named. The story is told in Ovid's *Fasti* 3.851ff. and in Boccaccio 4.48 where, as Lotspeich observes (p. 118), Aries is a symbol of the fruitfulness of spring.

6. **hent,** 'held', an archaism; though revived by early Tudor poets it was glossed by Speght.

7. **ysame,** 'together', a nonce-word, archaic in cast, obviously used for the sake of the metre.

33. April was identified with Venus, as in Ovid's *Fasti* 4.13ff. Its zodiacal sign was Taurus, here taken as the bull in whose shape Jove seduced Europa, carrying her out to sea. The story is told at the end of

Met. 2., where Ovid remarks that 'majesty and love go ill together'. The first stanzas of the pageant of the months are meant perhaps to discomfort Jove by alluding to his sexual exploits.

4. Argolick fluids, the waters of the Gulf of Argolis in the Aegean.

5. studs, an allusion to the stars of the constellation, or possibly a remembrance of Ovid's description of the horns 'more polished and shining than any jewel' in *Met.* 2.868.

34. May becomes a mayd by a play on words 'annominatio', by association with the seasonal festivities (see C. L. Barber, *Shakespeare's Festive Comedy* (1958), for a discussion of these), alluded to throughout the stanza, and by virtue of the month's association with Maia, mother of Mercury, whose 'house' is the sign of the zodiac. The tenderness Spenser associated with Maia can be seen in his *Epithalamion* 307–10. There are overtones here, as in the May festivities themselves, of a compliment to Elizabeth, the Virgin Queen.

4. brethren's, the Gemini, Castor and Pollux, twins of Leda, who had also been seduced by Jove. May was in their sign of the zodiac.

5. Like a queen of the May festivities. The Gemini were famed as athletes, and thus in harmony with the May games motif.

8. rauisht, 'entranced'.

35.2. player, 'actor'. The allusion here (possibly suggested by the May game motif above) is to the leaf-clothed savage man or Woodwose, a frequent figure in art and at aristocratic festivities; cf. John Nichols, *Progresses of Elizabeth* (1823), 1.494–8, 3.113–5, 131. He was a type of wood-spirit, related to Faunus.

3. wrought, 'worked'.

4. yrons, the plowshare and its coulter, the blade in front of it. The word is monosyllabic here.

5. crab, Cancer, the zodiacal sign of June. When the midsummer sun reaches this sign it begins an apparent retrograde or crab-like motion and descends obliquely.

7. yode, 'went'. A deliberate archaism, cf. McElderry, 152.

8–9. that . . . grace, hypocrites, from the Greek, meaning 'actor', and probably suggested by 2. Some editors find this an allusion to the puritans, see notes to *Variorum* 7.304–5. But Spenser may also be thinking of the fawning courtier backing away politely from his superiors.

36.2. The detail echoes Ovid, *Met.* 2.28, as Cumming, 248 shows.

3. The lyon is the zodiacal sign of July. Lotspeich, p. 118, notes that Spenser in *Daphnaida* 165–6 identifies the constellation with the Nemaean lion killed by Hercules, the son of Amphitryon (hence th' Amphitrionide), as the first of his labours.

7. him, 'himself', a common Elizabethan usage; see Abbott, p. 149.

8. sithe, 'sythe'.

37.3. Virgo is August's zodiacal sign, depicted in some classical sources as holding ears of corn.

6. The **mayd** is Astraea, the goddess of justice, who left earth after the end of the Golden Age at the time of the revolt of the Titans; see Ovid, *Met.* 1.140ff. Spenser may also have had in mind Comes' (2.8) identification of Astraea with Ceres. Elizabeth was frequently complimented under allusions to Astraea, as is probably the case here; see Yates, 'Elizabeth as Astraea', *Journal of the Warburg and Courtauld Institute* 10 (1947), esp. 65–70.

9. **extold,** 'raised'.

38.3. **boot,** 'prize'.

6. The knife-hook was used in harvesting fruit.

7–9. The constellation Libra, or Scales, symbolizes the equinox. This sign was associated with the function of justice, as was Virgo, with which it was often paired in classical times.

7. **assayle,** 'determine'.

9. **equall,** 'impartially'. **scann'd,** 'measured'.

39.2. **noule,** 'head'. **totty,** 'dizzy'. **must,** 'new wine'. These words are relatively rare, but not archaic, despite the possible recollection of Chaucer's *Reeve's Tale* 4253.

3. **wine-fats see,** the 'sea' of wine in the vats.

4. **gust,** 'taste'.

6–8. The zodiacal sign Scorpio. Spenser apparently follows Comes 8.22 here rather than classical versions; see Lotspeich, p. 94. According to Comes, Orion's boast of his hunting skill angered Diana, who hid a scorpion which killed Orion as he passed. In remorse Diana had both Orion and the scorpion translated to the heavens. See *Variorum* 7.306n.

40.1. **full.** The Newberry copy has 'full full', an obvious error.

5. **breem,** 'rough' or 'cold'. The precise meaning of the word is uncertain. It is a deliberate archaism. OED records a related meaning for 'brim' in the 1580s, but the word itself is found in Lydgate, used of winter, and in Chaucer, where F. N. Robinson (ed. 1933) glosses it as 'furious'.

7. The ellipsis of the nominative at the beginning of the line is common; see Abbott, pp. 399–402, and especially logical here.

9. Chiron, a wise and beneficent Centaur, was born of Saturn and Philyra, a water-nymph. The name **Nais** is a variant of the Greek generic noun *Naias,* meaning water-nymph. Sawtelle, *The Sources of Spenser's Classical Mythology* (1896), p. 53, thinks Spenser may be following Apollonius Rhodius, *Argonautica* 4.813, where Philyra is called a Naiad. Chiron is called **dreadfull** here because while they could represent Christ's double nature, as in the *Ovide Moralisé,* centaurs were more often taken as types of bestiality and lust, and 'un centaure tirante de l'arc est souvent un symbole du Malin qui attaque la vertue' (M. Nijhoff, *Iconographie de l'Art Profane* (1932), p. 108). Chiron's translation to the heavens as Sagittarius, the zodiacal sign, is mentioned in both Boccaccio and Comes.

41.5. **goat,** the constellation Capricorn. Lotspeich, p. 118, thinks Spenser is following the version in Comes 7.2. The young Jove is supposed to have been fed by a goat while hiding from Saturn. In some versions Amalthea, the 'Idaean mayd', is depicted as taking the form of a goat. The allusions to the manger story are not unintended. **rade,** 'rode' in the Newberry copy; the printer's error suggests the relative rarity of this metaplastic form of the preterite.

7. **Idaean,** mistakenly 'Iaean' in the Newberry copy; Amalthea was associated with Mount Ida.

8–9. An allusion to Christmas hospitality, and possibly also a recollection of the story that Amalthea's horn became the Cornucopia or horn of plenty. The stanza is a particularly subtle plaiting of myth, Christian allusion, and ethical implication.

42.2. **weeds,** 'clothes'.

3. **quell,** 'quail' or 'faint'.

8–9. **earth-pot steane,** 'earthen jar' or 'urn'. **Steane,** a nonce-word, is usually taken to mean 'stone', yet Upton suggests it is 'agreeable to the Belgic word "steen", a steen-pot . . . or urn'. January's sign is Aquarius, the water-bearer. The allusion to the **Romane floud** has not been satisfactorily explained; it is probably the Tiber. Perhaps Spenser is recalling here stanza 13 of his translation of Bellay's *Ruins of Rome,* in which the overflowing Tiber washes away the 'pride' of antique Rome; this would echo the lopping of the 'needlesse spray' of 7. Perhaps, as R. N. Ringler suggests, Spenser is recalling his *Visions of Bellay,* stanza 9, with its Saturn-like figure pouring a flood from an urn, again associated by Spenser with Roman history and symbolic decay.

43.3. **two fishes.** The sign of Pisces. Spence, quoted in *Variorum* 1.365, criticizes several of the months as not 'well-marked'. And, indeed, aside from the reference to Lent, the fish seem only decorative.

8. **burgein,** 'bud'.

44.2. **equall pase,** 'abreast'.

3–5. The horses, Lotspeich thinks, are a recollection of Comes, but they were commonplace, as Marlowe's use of the line from Ovid's *Amores* in *Faustus* 5.2.139 shows. Night's ugliness and veil are also commonplaces. Lotspeich thinks the mace suggests Claudian's *De Raptu Proserpina* 2.363.

6. **pight,** 'placed', an archaism employed by early Tudor poets.

7. **trace,** 'pass'.

9. **all,** 'altogether', cf. Abbott, p. 36. **beames,** pronounced as two syllables; here archaic, cf. Sugden, p. 10, and Abbott, p. 385.

45.2. **timely,** 'passing', as in *FQ* 1.4.4.9. In Hesiod, *Theog.* 901, the Hours are daughters of Jove and Themis (law). Spenser's alteration suggests he wanted to eliminate an allegorical 'meaning' that might be distracting here. Surely Mutabilitie would eliminate so gross a piece of evidence for the other side, despite her general insensitivity to the implications of her witnesses. **endewed,** 'endowed'.

4. The Hours were associated with the Graces in aristocratic entertainment, as Padelford points out in *Variorum* 7.309.

5. **forslack,** 'cause neglect of'; cf. **forslowe** in canto VI.16 above. The intensive prefix in both bases is an archaism used for metrical reasons. **fore-shewed,** 'ordained'. The prefix here is the anticipatory *fore*. The slowing down of time for amorous ends was a commonplace. Jove himself had ordered the Hours to unyoke the horses of the sun so that he could spend the equivalent of three nights in one begetting Hercules; apparently he was taking no chances on the Hours.

6. Homer, *Iliad* 5.749, makes the Hours the porters at heaven's gate.

8. **wake,** 'guard'.

46. For the rhetorical structure of this stanza, see Introd., 'Rhetoric'.

2. **seene,** 'imagined', cf. Milton's description of Death in *PL* 2.666ff.

4. **to weene,** an active infinitive with the force of the passive, as in Shakespeare, Sonnet 129: 'Savage, extreme, rude, cruel, not to trust'; see Abbott, p. 259.

47.9. **but,** 'that'. The word is used here in the 'preventive' sense, as commonly in Shakespeare after 'denying' and 'doubting', see Abbott, pp. 83–4.

48.3. **of,** 'by'; see Abbott, p. 112. **disseise,** 'deprive', a word with legal connotations; in the Newberry copy, 'disseife', an obvious printer's error.

5–6. Jove refers to Mutabilitie's own 'evidence' in stanza 45. But note the conception here of Time as resulting from the motion of heavenly bodies, of time as the 'mesure of mevying'. This implied distinction between the perdurable and the eternal is well expressed in Boethius; see W. Nelson, *Poetry of Edmund Spenser* (1963), p. 309. Neither Jove nor Mutabilitie has yet invoked the idea of eternity.

7. **vertue,** 'power'. **cell,** the religious overtones of the line are not unintended by Jove.

49.1. A Latinate construction; see also Abbott, p. 279, on ellipses in Elizabethan English.

2–5. As R. N. Ringler notes, there is an ironic reminder here of Corinthians 4.18: 'the things which are seen are temporal; but the things which are not seen are eternal'.

6–9. Mutabilitie's paramologia (admitting an opponent's point in order to overthrow his whole argument) answers Jove's in 4 of the previous stanza. It is significant that in the argument following, Mutabilitie omits her most telling evidence—the Nova of 1572. See note to Canto VII.24.1–2 above.

50.1. A compliment to Elizabeth is probably intended. Bur Mutabilitie is also employing the Ptolemaic (essentially the Babylonian, and then the Stoic) order of planets according to their distance from the earth; hence in sequence the moon, Mercury, Venus, the sun, Mars, Jupiter, and Saturn; see F. R. Johnson, p. 52. Alastair Fowler,

Spenser and the Numbers of Time (1964), p. 231, points out that the positions of Jupiter and Saturn are interchanged by Spenser. Although he admits the alteration might be 'merely in the interest of rhetorical emphasis', he argues that Spenser makes it to allow for a conformity with the idea of the planetary week (see pp. 232–3).

2. **you.** Some editors, following Birch (1751) suggest an emendation to 'yon', but perhaps we are to see Mutabilitie turning from Jove to Cynthia here, and then—**with ye**—to the whole assembly of gods.

3. **darling.** The idea of the Moon as Jove's favourite has no classical warrant; the compliment to Elizabeth continues.

4. The association of Cynthia (Diana) with Cynthus Hill is found in *FQ* 2.3.31, following Virgil, *Aeneid* 1.498–500.

5. **crake,** 'brag', from 'crake', a small harsh-voiced bird; strongly pejorative.

51.4. Not until Kepler's work on elliptical orbits (1609) could the notion of 'erratic' planetary movements, based on the primitive assumption of circular orbits, begin to be dispelled. See Introd., 'The Narratives', and F. R. Johnson. In the Introduction to *FQ* 5.8, Mars is singled out as 'amiss of all the rest'. It was actually in *De Motibus Stellae Martis* (1609) that Kepler demonstrated an elliptical planetary orbit.

6. **faire . . . darke.** Spenser here is punning (**faire** as 'beautiful' and 'shining'; **darke** as 'ugly' and 'not visible').

7. **Phoebus,** the sun. **lightsome is alone,** 'alone is radiant'.

8. **by the way.** 'in his course'.

52.1–6. See note to 51.4.

7. **spare,** 'dispense with'.

9. **cranks . . . crookes,** 'twists . . . bends'. The passage is sarcastic, as in **Sir** for Saturn.

53.1. **Dan,** 'Master', here satiric.

3. **misfare,** 'mishap'.

5–6. Lotspeich, p. 75, notes the various opinions of Jove's birthplace in Comes 2.1.

9. **other,** 'other possibility'.

54.2. **Vnlesse . . . be.** But this, in Mutabilitie's sense of **kingdome** of the sky, has just been denied by her. In Nature's sense, however, it is the case.

4–9. The **vertue** or influence of a planet in a given 'house' or division of the heavens, modified by other planets in 'houses' opposite or at oblique angles to it. **obliquid,** a Spenserian coinage, used only here.

55.2. **clerkes,** 'learned men'.

3. Spenser, like Mutabilitie, has little specific interest in astronomical controversies; cf. F. R. Johnson, p. 194.

5–6. 'On the Copernican system the sphere of fixed stars was supposed

to be motionless . . . its apparent movement . . . accounted for by
the daily rotation of the earth'; F. R. Johnson, p. 105. But Spenser
may be alluding also to the increasing attention being paid to changes
in the relative positions of individual stars and constellations.

7. **wizards,** 'scientists'. **saine,** 'say'.

8. Mutabilitie is saying here that those who themselves move must
love mutation, and therefore all moving things in fact show her the
love subjects show a lord. The idea is a remote allusion to the Platonic
notion of mutual love of god and creation, whose circling is an attempt
to remain as close as possible to its creator while yet in motion; cf.
C. S. Lewis, *The Discarded Image,* p. 114. The idea is employed by
Spenser in *An Hymn of Heavenly Love* 22–28. Needless to say, its
use here is a piece of arrogance on Mutabilitie's part.

56.3. **by transuerse,** 'haphazardly'.

4. **let,** 'prevent'.

5. As does Typhaeus' sister, Bellona, in Spenser's *Visions of Bellay*
15.8 (11.8 in the earlier version).

8. **addoom that,** 'decide what'; **addoom** is a coinage apparently for
metrical purposes.

9. Mutabilitie is still submissive even at this point.

57.2. See Sugden, p. 138, on this construction. The entire stanza is a
necessary and effective rhetorical pause.

2. **ne . . . to or fro,** 'neither to one nor the other'. **space,** 'time'.

7. **whether,** 'which'.

9. **doome,** 'judgment'.

58. The philosophical significance of this stanza and the next is
discussed in Introd., 'Popular Medieval and Renaissance Thought',
and in *Variorum* 7, Appendix I.

4. **first estate,** 'original condition'.

5. **dilate,** 'extend', 'develop'. In *Religio Medici*, Browne explains
dilation using the figure of the seed which 'dilates' into bud and flower
and finally to seed again.

7. **fate,** See note to canto VI.33–6.

9. **states.** See 4.

59.4–5. Upton cites 1 Corinthians 15.52 on the Day of Judgment.

6. **whist,** 'silenced', the only *OED* example of the usage here.

7. **see,** 'throne'.

9. **wist,** 'knew'.

CANTO VIII

1.1. **whyleare,** 'recent', an archaism.

9. **Short time,** 'brief', but with the added connotation of physical
or planetary time as distinct from divine time (eternity); see A. Kent

Hieatt, *Short Time's Endless Monument* (1960), for an elaborate discussion of the possible implications of the phrase.

2.5. **contrayr,** 'the opposite of'; a metaplastic change for metrical smoothness.

6. cf. canto VII.55.8. The rueful echo of Mutabilitie's crowning aphorism underlines a change of tone.

8–9. Editors emend the two occurrences of 'Sabboth' to 'Sabaoth', and 'Sabaoth' to 'Sabbaoth', following Upton's observation that in Romans 9.29 'Sabaoth' means 'armies' and 'Sabbaoth' 'rest'. D. C. Allen, *MLN* 64 (1949), defends the 1609 text as wordplay and as Spenser's prayer, not for 'rest', but for admission to the ranks of the Saints; cf. Friedland, *MLQ* 17 (1956).

APPENDIX I

The following extracts are from the Loeb Library edition of Boethius'
Consolation of Philosophy (1918) in the translation of I. T. (1609),
revised by H. F. Stewart. The portions included are Book III, metre
2; and Book IV, prose 6.

(A)

How the first reins of all things guided are
By powerful Nature as the chiefest cause,
And how she keeps, with a foreseeing care,
The spacious world in order by her laws,
And to sure knots which nothing can untie,
By her strong hand all earthly motions draws—
To show all this we purpose now to try
Our pliant string, our musick's thrilling sound.
Although the Libyan lions often lie
Gentle and tame in splendid fetters bound,
And fearing their incensed master's wrath,
With patient looks endure each blow and wound,
Yet if their jaws they once in blood do bathe,
They, gaining courage, with fierce noise awake
The force which Nature in them seated hath,
And from their necks the broken chains do shake;
Then he that tamed them first doth feel their rage,
And torn in pieces doth their fury slake.
The bird shut up in an unpleasing cage,
Which on the lofty trees did lately sing,
Though men, her want of freedom to assuage,
Should unto her with careful labour bring
The sweetest meats which they can best devise,
Yet when within her prison fluttering
The pleasing shadows of the groves she spies,
Her hated food she scatters with her feet,
In yearning spirit to the woods she flies,
The woods' delights do tune her accents sweet.
When some strong hand doth tender plant constrain
With his debased top the ground to meet,
If it let go, the crooked twig again
Up toward Heaven itself it straight doth raise.
Phoebus doth fall into the western main,
Yet doth he back return by secret ways,
And to the earth doth guide his chariot's race.
Each thing a certain course and laws obeys,
Striving to turn back to his proper place;
Nor any settled order can be found,
But that which doth within itself embrace
The births and ends of all things in a round.

(B)

'It is true,' quoth I, 'but since it is thy profession to explicate the causes of hidden things, and to unfold the reasons which are covered with darkness, I beseech thee vouchsafe to declare what conclusion thou drawest from these things, for this miracle troubleth me above all others.' Then she smiling a little said: 'Thou invitest me to a matter which is most hardly found out, and can scarcely be sufficiently declared; for it is such that, one doubt being taken away, innumerable others, like the heads of Hydra, succeed, neither will they have any end unless a man repress them with the most lively fire of his mind. For in this matter are wont to be handled these questions: of the simplicity of Providence; of the course of Fate; of sudden chances; of God's knowledge and predestination, and of free will; which how weighty they are, thou thyself discernet. But because it is part of thy cure to know these things also, though the time be short, yet we will endeavour to touch them briefly. But if the sweetness of verse delight thee, thou must forbear this pleasure for a while, until I propose unto thee some few arguments.' 'As it pleaseth thee,' quoth I.

Then taking as it were a new beginning, she discoursed in this manner: 'The generation of all things, and all the proceedings of mutable natures, and whatsoever is moved in any sort, take their causes, order, and forms from the stability of the Divine mind. This, placed in the castle of its own simplicity, hath determined manifold ways for doing things; which ways being considered in the purity of God's understanding, are named Providence, but being referred to those things which He moveth and disposeth, they are by the ancients called Fate. The diversity of which will easily appear if we weigh the force of both. For Providence is the very Divine reason itself, seated in the highest Prince, which disposeth all things. But Fate is a disposition inherent in changeable things, by which Providence connecteth all things in their due order. For Providence embraceth all things together, though diverse, though infinite; but Fate putteth every particular thing into motion being distributed by places, forms, and time; so that this unfolding of temporal order being united into the foresight of God's mind is Providence, and the same uniting, being digested and unfolded in time, is called Fate. Which although they be diverse yet the one dependeth on the other. For fatal order proceedeth from the simplicity of Providence. For as a workman conceiving the form of anything in his mind taketh his work in hand, and executeth by order of time that which he had simply and in a moment foreseen, so God by His Providence disposeth whatsoever is to be done with simplicity and stability, and by Fate effecteth by manifold ways and in the order of time those very things which He disposeth. Wherefore, whether Fate be exercised by the subordination of certain Divine spirits to Providence, or this fatal web be woven by a soul or by the service of all nature, or by the heavenly motions of the stars, by angelical virtue, or by diabolical industry, or by some or all of these, that certainly is manifest that Providence is an immoveable and simple form of those things which are to be done, and Fate a moveable connexion and temporal order of those things which the

Divine simplicity hath disposed to be done. So that all that is under Fate is also subject to Providence, to which also Fate itself obeyeth. But some things which are placed under Providence are above the course of Fate. And they are those things which nigh to the first Divinity, being stable and fixed, exceed the order of fatal mobility. For as of orbs which turn about the same centre, the inmost draweth nigh to the simplicity of the midst, and is as it were the hinge of the rest, which are placed without it, about which they are turned, and the outmost, wheeled with a greater compass, by how much it departeth from the middle indivisibility of the centre, is so much the more extended into larger spaces, but that which is joined and coupled to that middle approacheth to simplicity, and ceaseth to spread and flow abroad, in like manner that which departeth farthest from the first mind is involved more deeply in the meshes of Fate, and everything is so much the freer from Fate, by how much it draweth nigh to the hinge of all things. And if it sticketh to the stability of the Sovereign mind, free from motion, it surpasseth also the necessity of Fate. Wherefore in what sort discourse of reason is compared to pure understanding, that which is produced to that which is, time to eternity, a circle to the centre, such is the course of moveable Fate to the stable simplicity of Providence. That course moveth the heaven and stars, tempereth the elements one with another, and transformeth them by mutual changing. The same reneweth all rising and dying things by like proceeding of fruits and seeds. This comprehendeth also the actions and fortunes of men by an unloosable connexion of causes, which since it proceeds from the principles of unmovable Providence, the causes also must needs be immutable. For in this manner things are best governed, if the simplicity which remaineth in the Divine mind produceth an inflexible order of causes, and this order restraineth with its own immutability things otherwise mutable, and which would have a confused course. Whereof it ensueth that though all things seem confused and disordered to you, who are not able to consider this order, notwithstanding all things are disposed by their own proper measure directing them to good. For there is nothing which is done for the love of evil, even by the wicked themselves: whom, as hath been abundantly proved, lewd error carrieth away while they are seeking after that which is good, so far is it that order proceeding from the hinge of the Sovereign Goodness should avert any from his first beginning.

APPENDIX II

The following extract from Chaucer's *Parlement of Foulys* is from the edition by D. S. Brewer in this series. It runs from line 295 to line 329 and resumes at line 365, concluding at the end of the stanza.

Whan I was come aȝen into the place   295
That I of spak, that was so sote & grene,
Forth welk I tho, mynseluyn to solace.
Tho was I war wher that ther sat a queene,
That as of lyght the somer sunne shene
Passith the sterre, right so ouer mesure   300
She fayrere was than ony creature.

And in a launde, vpon an hil of flouris,
Was set this noble goddesse [of] Nature;
Of braunchis were here hallis & here bouris
Iwrought after here cast & here mesure,   305
Ne there was foul that comyth of engendrure,
That they ne weré prest in here presence,
To take hire dom, & ȝeue hire audyence.

For this was on seynt Valentynys day,
Whan euery bryd comyth there to chese his make   310
Of euery kyndé that men thynké may,
And that so heuge a noysé gan they make,
That erthe & eyr & tre & euery lake
So ful was, that onethé was there space
For me to stonde, so ful was al the place.   315

ƒ485v   And right as Aleyn in the *Pleynt of Kynde*
Deuyseth Nature *of* aray & face,
In swich aray men myghte hire theré fynde.
This nobil empéressé, ful of grace,
Bad euery foul to take his owené place,   320
As they were wonyd alwey from ȝer to ȝeere,
Seynt Valentynys day, to stondyn theere.

That is to seyn, the foulis of rauyne
Where heyest set, & thanne [the] foulis smale
That etyn as hem Nature wolde enclyne,   325
As werm or thyng [of whiche] I telle *no* tale;
And watyrfoul sat loueste in the dale;
But foul that lyuyth be sed sat on the grene,
And that so fele that wondyr was to sene.

         *   *   *

What shulde I seyn? Of foulys euery kynde   365
That in this world hath federis & stature
Men myghtyn in that place assemblede fynde
Byfore the noble goddesse [of] Nature;
And eueriche of hem dede his besy cure
Benygnely to chese, or for to take   370
By hire acord, his formel or his make.

APPENDIX III

The extract which follows is taken from Arthur Golding's translation of Ovid's *Metamorphoses* (1567). It follows fairly closely Pythagoras' speech in Book XIV of Ovid.

And forasmuch as God this instant howre

Dooth move my toong too speake, I will obey his heavenly powre.
My God *Apollos* temple I will set you open, and
Disclose the woondrous heavens themselves, and make you understand 160
The Oracles and secrets of the Godly majestye.
Greate things, and such as wit of man could never yit espye,
And such as have beene hidden long, I purpose too descrye.
I mynd too leave the earth, and up among the starres too stye,
I mynd too leave this grosser place, and in the clowdes too flye,
And on stowt *Atlas* shoulders strong too rest my self on hye,
And looking downe from heaven on men that wander heere and there
In dreadfull feare of death as though they voyd of reason were,
Too give them exhortation thus, and playnely too unwynd
The whole discourse of destinie as nature hath assignd. 170
O men amaazd with dread of death, why feare yee *Limbo Styx,*
And other names of vanitie, which are but *Poets* tricks?
And perrills of another world, all false surmysed geere?
For whither fyre or length of tyme consume the bodyes heere,
Yee well may thinke that further harmes they cannot suffer more.
For soules are free from death. Howbeet, they leaving evermore
Theyr former dwellings, are receyvd and live ageine in new.
For I myself (ryght well in mynd I beare it too be trew)
Was in the tyme of Trojan warre *Euphorbus, Panthewes* sonne,
Quyght through whoose hart the deathfull speare of *Menelay* did ronne. 180
I late ago in *Junos* Church at *Argos* did behold
And knew the target which I in my left hand there did hold.
All things doo chaunge. But nothing sure dooth perrish. This same spright ⎫
Dooth fleete, and fisking heere and there dooth swiftly take his flyght ⎬
From one place too another place, and entreth every wyght, ⎭
Removing out of man too beast, and out of beast too man.
But yit it never perrisheth nor never perrish can.
And even as supple wax with ease receyveth fygures straunge,
And keepes not ay one shape, ne bydes assured ay from chaunge,
And yit continueth alwayes wax in substaunce: So I say 190
The soule is ay the selfsame thing it was, and yit astray
It fleeteth intoo sundry shapes. Therfore least Godlynesse ⎫
Bee vanquisht by outragious lust of belly beastlynesse, ⎬
Forbeare (I speake by prophesie) your kinsfolkes ghostes too chace ⎭
By slaughter: neyther nourish blood with blood in any cace.
And sith on open sea the wynds doo blow my sayles apace,
In all the world there is not that that standeth at a stay.
Things eb and flow, and every shape is made too passe away.
The tyme itself continually is fleeting like a brooke.

For neyther brooke nor lyghtsomme tyme can tarrye still. But looke 200
As every wave dryves other foorth, and that that commes behynd
Bothe thrusteth and is thrust itself: Even so the tymes by kynd
Doo fly and follow bothe at once, and evermore renew.
For that that was before is left, and streyght there dooth ensew
Anoother that was never erst. Eche twincling of an eye
Dooth chaunge. Wee see that after day commes nyght and darks the sky,
And after nyght the lyghtsum Sunne succeedeth orderly.
Like colour is not in the heaven when all things weery lye
At midnyght sound a sleepe, as when the daystarre cleere and bryght
Commes foorth uppon his milkwhyght steede. Ageine in other plyght 210
The morning *Pallants* daughter fayre the messenger of lyght
Delivereth intoo *Phebus* handes the world of cleerer hew.
The circle also of the sonne what tyme it ryseth new
And when it setteth, looketh red, but when it mounts most hye,
Then lookes it whyght, bycause that there the nature of the skye
Is better, and from filthye drosse of earth dooth further flye.
The image also of the Moone, that shyneth ay by nyght,
Is never of one quantitie. For that that giveth lyght
Too day, is better than the next that followeth, till the full.
And then contrarywyse eche day her lyght away dooth pull. 220
What? seest thou not how that the yeere as representing playne
The age of man, departes itself in quarters fowre? first bayne
And tender in the spring it is, even like a sucking babe.
Then greene, and voyd of strength, and lush, and foggye is the blade,
And cheeres the husbandman with hope. Then all things florish gay.
The earth with flowres of sundry hew then seemeth for too play,
And vertue small or none too herbes there dooth as yit belong.
The yeere from springtyde passing foorth too sommer, wexeth strong,
Becommeth lyke a lusty youth. For in our lyfe through out
There is no tyme more plentifull, more lusty whote and stout. 230
Then followeth Harvest when the heate of youth growes sumwhat cold,
Rype, meeld, disposed meane betwixt a yoongman and an old,
And sumwhat sprent with grayish heare. Then ugly winter last
Like age steales on with trembling steppes, all bald, or overcast
With shirle thinne heare as whyght as snowe. Our bodies also ay
Doo alter still from tyme too tyme, and never stand at stay.
Wee shall not bee the same wee were too day or yisterday.
The day hath beene, wee were but seede and only hope of men,
And in our moothers woomb wee had our dwelling place as then,
Dame Nature put too conning hand and suffred not that wee 240
Within our moothers streyned womb should ay distressed bee,
But brought us out too aire, and from our prison set us free.
The chyld newborne lyes voyd of strength. Within a season tho
He wexing fowerfooted lernes like savage beastes too go.
Then sumwhat foltring, and as yit not firme of foote, he standes
By getting sumwhat for too helpe his sinewes in his handes.
From that tyme growing strong and swift, he passeth foorth the space
Of youth, and also wearing out his middle age a pace,
Through drooping ages steepye path he ronneth out his race.
This age dooth undermyne the strength of former yeeres, and throwes 250

t downe: which thing old *Milo* by example playnely showes.
'or when he sawe those armes of his (which heeretoofore had beene
as strong as ever *Hercules* in woorking deadly teene
Of biggest beastes) hand flapping downe, and nought but empty skin,
He wept. And *Helen* when shee saw her aged wrincles in
A glasse, wept also: musing in herself what men had seene,
That by twoo noble princes sonnes shee twyce had ravisht beene.
Thou tyme, the eater up of things, and age of spyghtfull teene,
Destroy all things. And when that long continuance hath them bit,
'ou leysurely by lingring death consume them every whit.   260
And theis that wee call Elements doo never stand at stay.
The enterchaunging course of them I will before yee lay.
Give heede thertoo. This endlesse world conteynes therin I say
'owre substances of which all things are gendred. Of theis fower
The Earth and Water for theyr masse and weyght are sunken lower.
The other cowple Aire and Fyre the purer of the twayne
Mount up, and nought can keepe them downe. And though there doo remayne
A space betweene eche one of them: yit every thing is made
Of themsame fowre, and intoo them at length ageine doo fade.
The earth resolving leysurely dooth melt too water sheere,   270
The water fyned turnes too aire. The aire eeke purged cleere
From grossenesse, spyreth up aloft, and there becommeth fyre.
From thence in order contrary they backe ageine retyre.
Fyre thickening passeth intoo Aire, and Ayër wexing grosse
Returnes to water: Water eeke congealing intoo drosse,
Becommeth earth. No kind of thing keepes ay his shape and hew.
For nature loving ever chaunge repayres one shape a new
Uppon another, neyther dooth there perrish aught (trust mee)
'n all the world, but altring takes new shape. For that which wee
Doo terme by name of being borne, is for too gin too bee   280
Another thing than that it was: And likewise for too dye,
Too cease too bee the thing it was. And though that varyably
Things passe perchaunce from place too place: yit all from whence they came
Returning, doo unperrisshed continew still the same.
But as for in one shape, bee sure that nothing long can last.

APPENDIX IV

The following stanzas are from Book III, Canto VI of *The Faerie Queene*, the famous Garden of Adonis passages. The text is that of the *Variorum* edition.

xxi

She brought her to her ioyous Paradize,
   Where most she wonnés, when she on earth does dwel.
   So faire a place, as Nature can deuize:
   Whether in *Paphos,* or *Cytheron* hill,
   Or it in *Gnidus* be, I wote not well;
   But well I wote by tryall, that this same
   All other pleasant places doth excell,
   And called is by her lost louers name,
The *Gardin* of *Adonis,* farre renowmd by fame.

xx

In that same Gardin all the goodly flowres,
   Wherewith dame Nature doth her beautifie,
   And decks the girlonds of her paramoures,
   Are fetcht: there is the first seminarie
   Of all things, that are borne to liue and die,
   According to their kindes. Long worke it were,
   Here to account the endlesse progenie
   Of all the weedes, that bud and blossome there;
But so much as doth need, must needs be counted here.

xxx

It sited was in fruitfull soyle of old,
   And girt in with two walles on either side;
   The one of yron, the other of bright gold,
   That none might thorough breake, nor ouer-stride:
   And double gates it had, which opened wide,
   By which both in and out men moten pas;
   Th'one faire and fresh, the other old and dride:
   Old *Genius* the porter of them was,
Old *Genius,* the which a double nature has.

xxxi

He letteth in, he letteth out to wend,
   All that to come into the world desire;
   A thousand thousand naked babes attend
   About him day and night, which doe require,
   That he with fleshly weedes would them attire:
   Such as him list, such as eternall fate
   Ordained hath, he clothes with sinfull mire,
   And sendeth forth to liue in mortall state,
Till they againe returne backe by the hinder gate.

xxxii

After that they againe returned beene,
   They in that Gardin planted be againe;
   And grow afresh, as they had neuer seene

Fleshly corruption, nor mortall paine.
Some thousand yeares so doen they there remaine;
And then of him are clad with other hew,
Or sent into the chaungefull world againe,
Till thither they returne, where first they grew:
So like a wheele around they runne from old to new.

Ne needs there Gardiner to set, or sow,   xxxiv
To plant or prune: for of their owne accord
All things, as they created were, doe grow,
And yet remember well the mightie word,
Which first was spoken by th'Almightie lord,
That bad them to increase and multiply:
Ne doe they need with water of the ford,
Or of the clouds to moysten their roots dry;
For in themselues eternall moisture they imply.

Infinite shapes of creatures there are bred,   xxxv
And vncouth formes, which none yet euer knew,
And euery sort is in a sundry bed
Set by it selfe, and ranckt in comely rew:
Some fit for reasonable soules t'indew,
Some made for beasts, some made for birds to weare,
And all the fruitfull spawne of fishes hew
In endlesse rancks along enraunged were,
That seem'd the *Ocean* could not containe them there.

Daily they grow, and daily forth are sent   xxxvi
Into the world, it to replenish more;
Yet is the stocke not lessened, nor spent,
But still remaines in euerlasting store,
As it at first created was of yore.
For in the wide wombe of the world there lyes,
In hatefull darkenesse and in deepe horrore,
An huge eternall *Chaos*, which supplyes
The substances of natures fruitfull progenyes.

All things from thence doe their first being fetch,   xxxvii
And borrow matter, whereof they are made,
Which when as forme and feature it does ketch,
Becomes a bodie, and doth then inuade
The state of life, out of the griesly shade.
That substance is eterne, and bideth so,
Ne when the life decayes, and forme does fade
Doth it consume, and into nothing go,
But chaunged is, and often altred to and fro.

The substance is not chaunged, nor altered,   xxxviii
But th'only forme and outward fashion;
For euery substance is conditioned
To change her hew, and sundry formes to don,

Meet for her temper and complexion:
For formes are variable and decay,
By course of kind, and by occasion,
And that faire flowre of beautie fades away,
As doth the lilly fresh before the sunny ray.

Great enimy to it, and to all the rest,   xxxix
    That in the *Gardin* of *Adonis* springs,
    Is wicked *Time*, who with his scyth addrest,
    Does mow the flowring herbes and goodly things,
    And all their glory to the ground downe flings,
    Where they doe wither, and are fowly mard:
    He flyes about, and with his flaggy wings
    Beates downe both leaues and buds without regard,
Ne euer pittie may relent his malice hard.

Yet pittie often did the gods relent,   xl
    To see so faire things mard, and spoyled quight:
    And their great mother *Venus* did lament
    The losse of her deare brood, her deare delight;
    Her hart was pierst with pittie at the sight,
    When walking through the Gardin, them she saw,
    Yet no'te she find redresse for such despight.
    For all that liues, is subiect to that law:
All things decay in time, and to their end do draw.

SELECT BIBLIOGRAPHY

Books and articles cited in the Introduction or Notes to make a particular point are not listed again here.

I. BIBLIOGRAPHICAL AND REFERENCE WORKS

ATKINSON, D. F., *Edmund Spenser: A Bibliographical Supplement* (1937).

CARPENTER, F. I., *A Reference Guide to Edmund Spenser* (1923).

McNEIR, W., and PROVOST, F., *Annotated Bibliography of Edmund Spenser, 1937–1960* (Duquesne Univ. Press, 1962).

WHITMAN, C. H., *A Subject-Index to the Poems of Edmund Spenser* (1919).

II. LIFE OF SPENSER

JUDSON, A. C., *The Life of Edmund Spenser* (1945). The standard biography, but incomplete on some points; see arts. cited in Introd., 'Life'.

III. EDITIONS

The Works of Edmund Spenser: A Variorum Edition, ed. E. Greenlaw, C. G. Osgood, F. M. Padelford, R. Heffner, 10 vols. (1932–1957). Definitive and indispensable.

JOHNSON, F. R., *Critical Bibliography of the Works of Spenser* (1933). Especially useful on early editions.

Among important editions of Spenser preceding the *Variorum* are those of R. Church (4 vols., 1758), J. Upton (2 vols., 1758), and T. J. Wise (6 vols., 1895–7). Among standard modern editions are the Oxford by H. C. Smith and E. De Selincourt (1 vol., 1912), and the Cambridge, by R. E. N. Dodge (1 vol., 1908). There are innumerable school texts including the *Cantos*.

IV. SOCIAL BACKGROUND

HARRISON, G. B., *Elizabethan Journals: 1591–1603* (3 vols., 1928–33). Day by day account of Elizabethan life.

LEE, S., ed., *Shakespeare's England* (2 vols., 1916). Still valuable as an introduction to the details of Elizabethan life.

WILSON, E. C., *England's Eliza* (1939). A study of the cult of Elizabeth in literature.

WILSON, J. D., ed., *Life in Shakespeare's England* (Pelican Books, 1944). Useful excerpts from contemporary sources.

V. LITERARY AND INTELLECTUAL BACKGROUND

(i) TEXTS

BOETHIUS, *The Consolation of Philosophy*, translated by I. T. (1609) and revised by H. Stewart (Loeb Library, 1918).

CHAUCER, *The Parlement of Foulys*, edited by D. S. Brewer (Nelson's Medieval and Renaissance Library, 1960).

LUCRETIUS, *The Nature of the Universe*, translated by R. Latham (Penguin Books, 1951).

OVID, *Metamorphoses*, translated by M. Innes (Penguin Books, 1961).

(ii) LITERARY BACKGROUND—STUDIES

BUSH, D., *Mythology and the Renaissance Tradition in English Poetry* (Minneapolis, 1932).

CURTIUS, E. R., *Europäische Literatur und lateinisches Mittelalter* (Bern, 1948); English translation, *European Literature and the Latin Middle Ages* (1953). Invaluable on *topoi* and style.

LEWIS, C. S., *The Allegory of Love* (1936). Indispensable.

LEWIS, C. S., *English Literature in the Sixteenth Century* (1954).

LOTSPEICH, H. G., *Classical Mythology in the Poetry of Edmund Spenser* (1932).

NELSON, W., ed., *Form and Convention in the Poetry of Edmund Spenser: Selected Papers from the Inglish Institute* (1961). An excellent collection of scholarly essays.

SMITH, HALLETT, *Elizabethan Poetry: A Study in Conventions, Meaning, and Expression* (1952).

TILLYARD, E. M. W., *The English Epic and its Background* (1954).

TUVE, R., *Elizabethan and Metaphysical Imagery* (1947).

(iii) INTELLECTUAL BACKGROUND—STUDIES

ALLEN, D. C., *Doubt's Boundless Sea: Skepticism and Faith in the Renaissance* (1964).

BUSH, D., *The Renaissance and English Humanism* (1939). A good introduction to the period.

CRAIG, H., *The Enchanted Glass: the Elizabethan Mind in Literature* (1936).

ELLRODT, ROBERT, *Neoplatonism in the Poetry of Spenser* (Geneva, 1960).

HARRIS, V., *All Coherence Gone* (1949). A study of the idea of the world's decay.

JOHNSON, F. R., *Astronomical Thought in Renaissance England* (1937).

KRISTELLER, P. O., *Renaissance Thought* (Harper Torchbooks, 1961).

LEWIS, C. S., *The Discarded Image: An Introduction to Medieval and Renaissance Literature* (1964). Invaluable for understanding 'popular' commonplaces.

PATRIDES, C. A., 'Renaissance and Modern Thought on Last Things', *Harvard Theological Review* LI (1958).

SEZNEC, J., *The Survival of the Pagan Gods*, trans. B. Sessions (Harper Torchbooks, 1961).

TILLYARD, E. M. W., *The Elizabethan World Picture* (1944).

WINNY, J., ed., *The Frame of Order: An Outline of Elizabethan Belief Taken from Treatises of the Late Sixteenth Century* (1957).

WHITAKER, V. K., *The Religious Basis of Spenser's Thought* (1950).

WOODHOUSE, A. S. P., 'Nature and Grace in *The Faerie Queene*' *ELH* 16 (1949), 194–228.

VI. STUDIES OF SPENSER AND THE CANTOS

ARTHOS, J., *On the Poetry of Spenser and the Form of Romances* (1956).

BRADNER, L., *Edmund Spenser and 'The Faerie Queene'* (1948). A sensible introduction to the poet.

DAVIS, B. E. C., *Edmund Spenser, a Critical Study* (1933).

HAMILTON, A. C., *The Structure of Allegory in 'The Faerie Queene'* (1961).

HOUGH, GRAHAM, *A Preface to 'The Faerie Queene'* (1962).

JONES, H. S. V., *Spenser Handbook* (1930). Out of date in many respects, but still a useful guide.

MUELLER, W., ed., *Spenser's Critics: Changing Currents in Literary Taste* (1959).

NELSON, W., *The Poetry of Edmund Spenser* (1963).

RENWICK, W. L., *Edmund Spenser: an Essay on Renaissance Poetry* (1925). Useful criticism.

WATKINS, W. B. C., *Shakespeare and Spenser* (1950). Valuable contrasts illuminating Spenser's style and the *Mutabilitie Cantos*.

VII. TECHNICAL STUDIES

RIX, H. D., *Rhetoric in Spenser's Poetry* (Pennsylvania College Studies no. 7, 1940).

RUBEL, V., *Poetic Diction in the Renaissance from Skelton through Spenser* (1941).

JOSEPH, SISTER MIRIAM, C.S.C., *Shakespeare's Use of the Art of Language* (1947). An excellent introduction to Elizabethan rhetoric.

SUGDEN, H. W., *The Grammar of Spenser's 'Faerie Queene'* (Linguistic Society of America, 1936).